THE UNIVERSE

IS AT YOUR COMMAND

Vibrating the Creative Side of God

JEREMY LOPEZ

The Universe Is At Your Command: Vibrating the Creative Side of God

Copyright © 2018, Jeremy Lopez

Published by Identity Network

P.O Box 383213

Birmingham, AL 35238

www.IdentityNetwork.net

IDENTITY NETWORK

ENDORSEMENTS

"You are put on this earth with incredible potential and a divine destiny. This powerful, practical man shows you how to tap into powers you didn't even know you had" – Brian Tracy, Author of *The Power of Self-Confidence*

"He has drawn from the wells of his prophetic anointing very insightful revelation for us today. Securing the reader in a fortress of truth." – Roberts Liardon

"It is a transformational book that challenges you to rethink what you have been taught while reflecting more deeply upon the truth you have come to know. The journey through this book is prophetic, mystical, and magical, as you come to know who you really are for all eternity." – Robert Ricciardelli, Founder of The Converging Zone   Network

CONTENTS

FOREWORD

Do you remember what it was like, watching the worlds being formed? I was there. And you were there, also. How marvelous and truly exciting it was to watch, as the Creator first placed his brush upon the canvas which had only moments before seemed to be such a great and vast empty nothingness. Then, in an instant, the light came. Instinctively, as we watched the wondrous, luminous sight, we knew that nothing would ever be the same again. You and I watched as the worlds were formed – as beautiful planets of all manner were flung throughout the darkness, hanging, perfectly suspended with nothing to hold them in their places except the mind and the focused intention of the Creator. We looked on, eagerly, as Earth was formed, and somehow we all knew that it was a turning point. You and I listened and watched, excitedly, as the Creator reached down with his own hands – into the mud and into the dirt of the terrain below – and fashioned man. Remember how the Creator had told us that the man would be just like us? Made in our image and in our likeness? Finally, the time came when we, ourselves, would incarnate into human flesh. A new journey began. And somehow along the way, we became forgetful. Somewhere along the way, you and I forgot so very much. We forgot who we truly are – eternal, powerful, *thinking* spirits. We then found ourselves, here, in a world that we know, in some way, is not our true home.

The forgetfulness seemed like such a curse. And then Jesus came. Thankfully.

He reminded us of the glory we shared with him and with the Father. Then, as the Sprit came, with him came a great reminder of our true identity. And then awakening came. Oh, how we had longed for that awakening – the untethering of our minds from the cloud of forgetfulness. We remembered who we have always been – powerful co-creators who form worlds and attract our very desires with our very thoughts. My friend, today, in case you have forgotten, I wish to lovingly and gently remind you of your true identity as Creator. You existed with Him – within Him. In case you have forgotten, I wish to lovingly and gently remind you just how much power you truly possess. You seem to have forgotten. You are not a victim of this world. All of Heaven and all that is within this universe are at your command.

CASE FOR CREATION

As the Spirit of God moved upon the face of the deep, over a sea of vast and empty nothingness, there was a sense of great anticipation, and the very intention within the heart of the Godhead was revealed outwardly. As those first words were spoken, the heart of God was revealed – it was the heart of a creator. Oh, how indescribable that instant was, as the power of the Spirit, that great architect of the Divine Mind, uttered those first words into the cosmos that would soon appear: "Let there be light." Just as much as it is within the very essence of God to heal and to save and to deliver, it is equally, if not even more so, the nature of God to create at will, for the purpose of His own good pleasure. Yet, as a painter envisions a finished work long before his brush is ever placed upon the canvas and as a sculptor envisions within the mind's eye the masterpiece that is to be, long before the chisel is ever placed upon stone, so too did the magnificence of creation exist long before the words, "Let there be," were ever spoken. The eternal Divine thrust of creation existed within the heart of the Creator long before the words were ever uttered. Creation existed, firstly, within the heart of God.

As I write these words to you, now, more than ever before, I feel within my spirit a hunger which I have never known before. There exists within me an unction which has overtaken my life. In no uncertain terms, I long for the whole of humanity to come into the knowledge of the power of creation. I yearn for humanity to awaken to the realization that just as the force of creation existed within the mind of a loving Creator, so too does the power of creation exist within the mind and heart of each man. As I write these words to you, I bear my soul, as transparently as I know how. I now find myself living a life that many will only dream of. I say that not with pride or to make boast but, rather, to say that I know, firsthand, the

pg. 3

power of the creative mind of God. Above all, I know, firsthand, the power of the creative mind of man. The mind of God is the mind of man, and there is truly no separation or distance. I have given my entire life to the study and the teaching of the universal laws, mysteries, and divine principles of God. However, now, as never before, I find myself often times so very weighted by the heaviness of the creative power of God and I hear the voice of the Spirit daily saying, "Humanity must awaken to its *own* creative power."

The principles and revelatory knowledge contained within these pages serve as a testament not only to the power of a creative mind but also to the universal and divine principles which have been enacted within our world since the Creator first began to create. Now, in this season of my life, I am being called upon to deliver to humanity a great reminder. So very often in my ministry travels and within my coaching sessions, I hear of the agony and the pain experienced by so many beautiful souls who have yet to awaken to their own creative power. Even as I write these words, I can so very vividly feel the intense anguish and heartbreak so very evident within their lives. Many exude a pain and a discouragement that can quite literally be felt by all who encounter them. Quite often, with tears streaming down their faces, they approach me and ask for prayers of deliverance and inquire what the Word of the Lord is for their lives. "I feel cursed," many say. They go on to explain how, for generations, there has existed within their lives nothing but apparent lack and confusion. "When I pray, it never happens," they exclaim. These beautiful souls explain to me in very vivid detail how unfortunate event after unfortunate event plagues their lives and how, according to a word given to them by other so-called "prophets," they had seemingly been "hexed," in some way, destined to forever be the victim of a demonic curse of lack and confusion. Instantly, though, I know by the Spirit of God the true source of the issue, and the Holy Spirit speaks to me these words: "The only *curse* which exists is the mind which has not been renewed."

The *curse* is very real, my friend; however, it has very little do with malevolent entities or with works of darkness outside of ourselves and has absolutely everything to do with the darkness within – a mindset that has yet to be awakened to its own creative power. "For this purpose was the Son of God manifested, that he might destroy the works of the devil." (1 John 3:8)   As I look into the eyes of these individuals throughout the world, individuals so very desperate for answers and for change and relief, by the Holy Spirit, I know that I am not looking into the eyes of those troubled by darkness or by the demonic. No, I am looking into the eyes of souls who have simply become disconnected and disjointed, dismembered, within their own thoughts. I often embrace them and say to them, simply, "Remember." In those moments, the deep truly calls unto the deep. The deep within me begins to call unto the deep of them, encouraging them to remember their own creative power and to awaken to their own limitless potentiality in Christ by understanding their own true nature – the nature of a creator. Now, within this season, more now than at any time before, the Spirit is calling all flesh to begin to remember, or "re-member," coming back into alignment with the internal, innate power of the creative force.

pg. 8

My friend, I say to you, you are not now nor have you ever been the mere product of coincidental happenstance within the universe around you. Oh, how I long for you to recognize this Divine truth. You, rather, are the creator of the world around you. "For as he thinketh in his heart, so is he." (Proverbs 23:7) This passage of scripture has not only much to do with the revelatory knowledge of the power of our creative thoughts, but also has literally everything to do with our very nature as creators within the universe. My friend, may I share with you a secret that will not only revolutionize your life but will cause you to instantly begin to enter into the fullness of all that God has intended for you in all facets of your life? The

pg. 9

very universe is at your beck and call. The universe is at your command. It always has been. It always will be. I know that even as you read these words, you think to yourself, "How is that possible?" You also ask, "What about Jesus?" So often, I find so many authentic and genuine individuals continuing to pray fervent and heartfelt prayers for blessing and abundance; yet, they so often find very little result and, quite often, very little, if any, manifestation of the desires of their hearts ever seems to come. So, you would ask, "What about Jesus?" Well, I will tell you, my friend, quite simply. "As he is, so are we in this world." (I John 4:17) As Jesus is, so are you, in this world. Did Jesus, himself, not say in John

10:34, when directing them to remember the words of the written law, God said to certain leaders of the people, "You are gods?" The Hebrew word translated "gods" in Psalm 82:6 is *Elohim*. Interestingly enough, the term *Elohim* is translated as "judges" in Exodus 21:6, 22:8, 9, and 28. Oh, if you would receive this revelatory knowledge into your spirit today, never again will you question your own creative power. You see, the God of creation, He whose very essence is the very power of creation is the judge of all things, just as you are.

Did you know that within each and every moment of life you are constantly within your heart making a judgement of the creation you are enacting? Allow me to say it another way. Through your experiences, you are able to judge the creation of your life. When God created the intention of His heart, he acknowledged that His creation was "good." Can you, as a creator, say the same about the life you are creating? Is it good? Are you awakening each morning to a life that feels good? How does it feel? If it does not feel good then the Word of the Lord to you today is that you can begin to create again and begin anew today. You do this by first recognizing that you are, indeed, the creator of your own life experiences. Yes, Jesus saves; however it is up to you to renew the mind, daily. How often have we made excuses in an attempt to escape the personal responsibility of renewing the mind? "Lord, take this bondage away from me," we pray. "God, deliver me from the curse of lack." "Lord, bless me with abundance." My friend, I learned long ago that there is divine, supernatural power in personal responsibility.

Did you know that as a powerful spirit being, here, incarnated into the earth realm to have a human experience, you have absolutely no choice but to create? It is a divine fact. The very moment you incarnate into the human form to have this earthly experience, you begin to think and with each thought you begin to attract and to create your life experience. As I said in my book, *Abandoned to Divine Destiny*, "You are and always have been an eternal spirit, full of destiny and purpose." Not only are you a powerful, speaking spirit, more importantly, you are a powerful *thinking* spirit whose thoughts are at all times the very gauge by which you determine if the creation of your life is "good" or "bad." Yet, how very often have we, here within the earth realm, so soon forgotten the creative power which we possess? We pray for emotional healing, yet continue to dwell upon the negative emotions of seasons long-since passed which bring only destruction and disease upon us. We pray for financial increase and for the blessing of the Lord, yet never take the first step of faith in order to give birth to the dream of beginning the new business. We pray for

pg. 14

divine healing yet continue to fill our bodies –
the earthly temple – with processed and refined
foods and sugars which only bring decay and
rot. You see, we very rarely want to take
personal responsibility with our creative power.
"Let God handle it," we seem to casually say.
As a result, the earth is filled with sincere but
lazy individuals who have no experience within
the supernatural realm of God, who gather
within church buildings on Sunday to preach to
the world a power that they have yet to truly
experience for themselves. Is it any wonder
many throughout the world are so very turned
off by the hypocrisy of our organized religions?
I mean, can we blame them? All of humanity is
looking for the real.

pg. 15

"For the earnest expectation of the creature waiteth for the manifestation of the sons of God." (Romans 8:19) My friend, all of creation is looking for the moment when the creator – you – recognizes the power within to create the life God ordained and established and decreed for your life before time ever began. However, the word of God, in and of itself, does absolutely nothing and is powerless if there is no agreement. It hurts the religious mind to hear those words, does it not? To realize that the literal – or *letter* – of the Word is not enough to bring about change within this dimension? Do you not recall that even Jesus, himself, said religious tradition nullifies and makes void the Word of God? In fact, quite often, he could do

pg. 16

no miracles in select settings because of religious tradition and unbelief. "Making the word of God of none effect through your tradition, which ye have delivered," quite literally means that creation always requires agreement and partnership. Perhaps you have been taught, as we all were in some times passed, that words have power. I say to you, however, that it is the belief behind words which give them power. "A good man out of the good treasure of his heart brings forth good: and an evil man out of the evil treasure of his heart brings forth evil. For out of the abundance of his heart his mouth speaks." (Luke 6:45) It is the heart that thinks, my friend. So very often, we have battled others and even have battled ourselves over things such as terminology and word usage. We have waged countless wars and entered, quite often, into many useless debates, over the meanings of words. We do this because we value our tradition more than we value the revelation of the Spirit and the revelatory knowledge found within the Word of God. In fact, show me a believer who wishes to argue over terminology and I will show you a believer who has yet to awaken to the greater truths of the universal principles of God. Yes, you read that correctly, my friend.

If we as the Body of Christ are ever to fully come into the manifestation of greater works, in order to create the lives God intended, then we must first begin to look far beyond words and see into the thoughts and intentions and emotions of our own hearts. As very difficult and possibly painful as it is to hear, you and you, alone, are responsible for the creation of your life experiences, based entirely upon your thoughts. It is a proven, scientific fact that within all things, even now in this moment, there exists within all things a very real "God particle." In other words, the very creative nature of God is even now at work within all things. You might say, "Jeremy, that sounds so very 'new age.'" You say, "That seems like nothing more than a form of Spiritualism." However, in Colossians 1:17, did the Apostle Paul not write, "And he is before all things, and

pg. 19

by him all things consist?" With each and every thought you are attracting to you the life you now see. With each moment of thought or meditation you are manifesting thought forms into the earth realm. So often in my coaching sessions, many say to me, "Jeremy, I'm not creating the life I truly want for myself." I say with all love and all grace that such a statement is in no way correct. You see, you are always creating something, my friend. So the truth of the matter is not that you are not creating the life you want but, rather, that you *are* creating the life you do *not* want. Within the revelatory knowledge contained within the pages of this book, you will soon discover the reasons why and what you, as a powerful thinking spirit, can do, today, to begin to change the creation around you. Truly, the universe is at your beck and call. All things are at your command.

Although Jesus came to redeem you from the curse of the law, there are at all times universal laws which God himself placed into operation long before the beginning of time and you will never escape these laws of the universe. There is, in fact, a very real "Law of Attraction" at work within your daily life, even now. You say, "Jeremy, I've heard it all before." Well, therein lies the root of the issue. Why then are you not awakening to the truth of the universal law of God? As mystical as the "Law of Attraction" may seem to the religious

pg. 21

mindset, I encourage you to begin to move beyond terminology and into the truth of the principle. In other words, stop focusing upon the terms and begin to focus upon the Divine truth behind the terms. As Shakespeare famously said, "That which we call a rose, by any other word would smell as sweet." Words have very little meaning, in and of themselves. The power lies solely within the beliefs and thoughts behind those words. Quantum physics has much to say about the very nature of God. It's true that science only confirms and proves the existence of the Holy Spirit and of the Divine Mind of God. We, as individuals, must never fear the use of terminology. Religion does nothing but divides us from others and, above all, separates and divides our minds from our true and authentic creative nature. There are issues that you must begin to rethink. There are matters which you must begin to question.

There is a creative mind – the very creative mind which manifested the universe into existence with mere thought – which must be awakened. "And that, knowing the time, that now it is high time to awake out of sleep: for now is our salvation nearer than when we believed." (Romans 13:11) As "new age" as the term "awakening" may seem to the religious mind, rest assured, my friend, there will be no power without it. Do not be deceived. You have been deceived for far too long. The time

pg. 23

to awaken is now. The time to begin creating within the earth the very nature of God is today. As a man skilled in the prophetic arts for most of my life, I have had the tremendous honor of speaking into the lives of world leaders, heads of business, and heads of state. I have delivered the Word of the Lord to single mothers and to stars of the stage and screen. I have offered words of prophetic knowledge to men who have bankrupted and also to men who have built literal empires within the world of business. One thing I know beyond the shadow of any doubt is that it is the mind which creates the life we desire and also the life we do not desire. It is with our thoughts that we find either our success or our failure – either the blessing or the curse. The Word of the Lord, alone, is not the answer and no matter how well acquainted you are with the scriptures and regardless of how well-intentioned you may very well be within the practice of your religion, the issue is not the Word of the Lord but, rather, what you *think* about the Word of the Lord, which makes all the difference in the world.

Nothing is more wondrous and, quite frankly, equally as frightening as the Word of the Lord given to us through Hosea. "My people are *destroyed* for lack of *knowledge*: because thou hast rejected knowledge, I will also reject thee, that thou shalt be no priest to me: seeing thou hast forgotten the law of thy

God, I will also forget thy children." (Hosea 4:6) Yes, the generational curse is very real, and it is based in the mindset which refuses to acknowledge the laws of God. Just as there is a "Law of Sowing and Reaping," there is also the "Law of Attraction." It is the basis of all that is in operation within our world. As a prophet of God, the Divine mandate of God upon my life is to bring the church – more so, the whole of humanity – into the truth of the laws of God. "Howbeit when he, the Spirit of truth, is come, he will guide you into all truth: for he shall not speak of himself; but whatsoever he shall hear, that shall he speak: and he will shew you things to come." (John 16:13) My friend, in this season of your life, do you not think it is time

pg. 26

for you to begin living the life God intended? A life of abundance, increase, and Divine prosperity? I've been asked before if I consider myself a "prosperity preacher." Well, the truth is that in your life you will create either prosperity or lack. There is no in-between. So, why not choose prosperity?

MYSTERIES OF ATTRACTION

In no uncertain terms, it is one of the most successful and highly-sought books of all time and it really isn't difficult to see why. When Rhonda Byrne released her bestselling book, *The Secret*, audiences worldwide flocked to the teaching in an effort to discover what had been packaged as the secret to success. Like never before, it seemed that all of humanity was beginning to awaken to the power of the mind in a new and refreshing way. In the arena of self-help and spirituality, it seemed that something innovative, fresh, and new had arrived upon the scene. However, as someone who has devoted his entire life to the study of the principles and cycles of God found within the scriptures, the principles contained within the book were nothing new to me. In fact, I had been utilizing the *secret* for much of my life, within my own business, my travels, and my ministry. Truthfully, it was the reason that I had found the success and abundance I now enjoy and have the opportunity to experience daily. In *The Secret*, the author defines the true secret as the "Law of Attraction." A best-selling book quickly became a best-selling, highly acclaimed film, and the masses continued to hunger for more. All around the globe, highly successful men and women, successful self-motivated entrepreneurs, began to flock to herald and support the principles found within the book. Many openly expressed how it was the principles contained within the book which had built their empires and helped to amass their vast wealth. As a student of the prophetic, the principles contained within the book resonated within me – there was a familiarity, of sorts. There was a kindred spirit that I felt to those who had used or who had begun to put into practice the principles of the "Law of Attraction," because I knew, instinctively, that the principle is a very real law of Christ.

However, to my amazement, I also began to see many Bible-believing Christians and those of the religious persuasion flock to openly condemn the book. Many began to openly boycott its sale, heralding it as nothing more than "new age" material or a repackaged, reformatted brand of Spiritualism. "This is heresy," I heard many say. "Where does Jesus fit into this teaching?" Others went as far as to call the source material nothing more than witchcraft and the conjuring of demons. For some, the "Dark Ages" never truly ended, it seems. Why are we so fixated upon the usage of certain words and terms? Why do we choose to be defined by terminology and words upon a page? As I said within my book, *Abandoned to*

Divine Destiny, "We must recognize that words are limiting things – we must dance around their inadequacies, hedging our bets at what will and will not be said or heard. Words, best understood, are little more than houses we construct to shelter the realities that live within them." Words, in and of themselves, are meaningless. It is the mind and the intention which gives meaning to spoken or written words. For centuries, the Jewish culture had lived by the written and the spoken word based upon the Mosaic Law of the old covenant. To say that Judaism had become legalistic, in our modern interpretation of the term *legalism*, would be quite the understatement. There was knowledge of the written and spoken words;

pg. 33

however, there was no revelatory unction. There was no spiritual understanding. There was only outward practice and ritualistic work. Then, in the fullness of time, the Word became flesh and dwelt among us, and we beheld the very essence of the artistic creator. Still, though, for those who had for so long been so fixated upon the written and spoken words, the teachings of the man, Jesus, seemed far too heretical – too extreme.

I often think to myself that the Pharisees and the religious elite of the day would have probably referred to Jesus as "new age," also. However, in no uncertain terms, a very new age had dawned and with it, the ushering in of revelatory knowledge and spiritual truth. An opportunity for awakening had come to humanity. Now, millennia later, we find ourselves within a time not unlike that time – a time in which we find ourselves still battling each other over the usage of written and spoken words and chosen terminology. Much like that time, we reject the power of the Spirit because what we see or hear in no way seems to align with our own preconceived, legalistic interpretations of what the words should represent. In truth, it in no way matters if you choose to accept the terminology of the "Law of Attraction," my friend; it in no way negates that you are operating within the principle even now, as you read the pages of this book. Each and every morning you arise to meet a new day and, perhaps more so, even while you're sleeping, you are thinking and your mind is in total operation. With each thought, you are creating *something*.

It's been said before that when you change your thoughts you change your life. I know this to be true. You could not even imagine the abundance and the prosperity that I enjoy each and every day of my life because I learned long ago the necessity of mixing visualization and meditation with my prayers. In truth, God isn't concerned with whether you call the principles behind the creative process "The Law of Attraction," "The Secret," or anything else. The terminology changes nothing at all. Before the worlds were ever spoken into existence, there were Divine laws being enacted. How many blessings have we missed out on simply because they were presented with words we didn't like? How often have you, in your life, created a world that wasn't satisfying to you, simply because you said, and "I don't believe that"? Your unbelief does not stop the creative flow of the Divine Mind; it merely creates for you a life opposite the intended effect. "For what if some did not believe? Shall their unbelief make the faith of God without effect?" (Romans 3:3) You see, there is a creative process ongoing at all times, and you are a part of that process right now,

pg. 37

although you might not recognize it yet. A powerful thinking spirit, which you are, has no choice but to create. There is no escaping the "Law of Attraction," regardless what you choose to call it. I know a man who is heavily involved within the practice of Spiritualism, who identifies himself as a "medium" and also teaches his clients the principles of the "Law of Attraction." Although I in no way align myself with such works or condone such occultic practice because of what scripture teaches, he and I agree, wholeheartedly, that the mind is constantly creating. You see, the principles of the Spirit are always at work, regardless of what we choose to call them and regardless of what we choose to call ourselves.

pg. 38

Think of this for a moment, my friend. Have you ever found yourself wondering why it is that some are truly successful and able to accomplish great things and build wealth while others, seemingly, struggle daily just to survive? Even more, have you ever wondered why some of the most devout believers, who truly are passionate about Christ, do without while so many others who in no way even study the scriptures find great success and seem to possess the "Midas Touch?" Well, the answer is very simple, as offensive as it may be to the religious mindset. The principles of the universe are always in play. "That ye may be the children of your Father which is in heaven: for he maketh his sun to rise on the evil and on

pg. 39

the good, and sendeth rain on the just and on the unjust." (Matthew 5:45) I cannot stress enough, my friend; the principles of the universe are always in play, at all times. In my travels throughout the world all these years, I have seen, firsthand, very sincere believers long for a power that they have yet to truly experience. Oh, how my heart burns and hungers for the awakening of humanity to its full creative power. Should not the church possess the power rather than the worldly? Should not the church - those armed with the truth of God - not even more so possess the power of creation, rather than the worldly or those who do not recognize the Spirit in operation? Why, then, is it this way? Because of the mind which has not been fully awakened to the power of creation.

My staff and I often marvel at just how quickly we now witness the "Law of Attraction" in motion. Often, within my own, personal life, I now find myself manifesting thought forms within the day or within the week, after first beginning to visualize them. I teach many of these principles in my course, *School of the Law of Attraction*, and I am seeing so many now putting these principles into action within their own lives. Day after day, thousands of testimonies pour into the offices of Identity Network from literally all across the globe. Many are now saying, "Jeremy, I tried it and it worked." In fact, just the other day, a woman responded to our offices after obtaining my teaching course, *School of Visualization*, and expressed, "After hearing the teaching, *Connecting to Creation Resources*, I now have launched my very own business and have attracted more money in three months than I made all last year!" All thanks to God for such miraculous changes. As I so often find myself saying to my audiences, "The work begins with you. It begins with the renewing of the mind." Remember, universal truth will forever be more important than terminology. We will either worship God – the Christ within – or we will worship words. Memorization is a very powerful tool for visualization, and I

pg. 42

wholeheartedly endorse the memorization of scripture. However, you can memorize and quote scripture until the cows come home and never see any change or the resulting, corresponding manifestation of those scriptures, if you do not set your mind to understanding the deeper mysteries found behind the words. The scriptures are filled with various names of God – names which, in some way, give us a glimpse into the nature and the essence of the Divine. When Moses asked for the name of God, he was given two powerful words: "I AM." (See Exodus 3:14) I share much more of this truth concerning one's identity in my book, *The Power of the Eternal Now*, but, suffice it say, even in that account, God was revealing himself to humanity as a creator.

In order to attract what we truly desire, we must, first, begin to recognize that words, both written and spoken, are merely outward projections of a deeper thought and intent, for as Jesus taught in Luke 6:45, it is the heart behind the words which truly matters. Knowing this, how very fascinating to then read the words of Jesus found in Matthew 12:36: "But I say unto you, That every idle word that men shall speak, they shall give account thereof in the day of judgment." There, again, is the idea of judgment. What if I were to say to you that in every moment you have placed emphasis upon your outward words and terminology or upon written words, rather than upon your own thoughts and the truth behind words, you have placed your own self into judgement of your creative power, without ever really being aware of it? Words, so often, can become much more than idle words; they can, quite literally, become our "idols." Freedom is in truth, alone. "And ye shall know the truth, and the truth shall make you free." (John 8:32) Recognize that truth, alone, does not free anyone: truth must be known. In other words, truth must be awakened to. In this season of my life, few things bring me greater joy and satisfaction than seeing individuals break free from their old patterns and paradigms of thinking – stepping forth into

pg. 45

a new, "now" season of their lives. When people begin to recognize the principles behind attracting, they begin to not only recognize how easily enacted the process can become, but they can begin to even find enjoyment in it!

Recognizing the principle of attraction is the first step in embarking upon a very Divine adventure in your life. Please hear me when I say to you that the true power lies within your intention, and your true intention will always reveal itself and make itself known. Don't believe that? Allow me to give an example of what I mean in an effort to better explain this truth. When a friend or acquaintance, in passing or when leaving, smiles and nonchalantly says,

"Love ya," that is in no way the same as when your spouse, or significant other, or romantic interest looks you in the eyes and says to you, "I love you." Though the words are quite similar and the semantics appear to be quite the same upon the surface level, the feeling is much different, is it not? In other words, the feeling or the power *behind* the words is what truly matters. It is the feeling which is manifesting the true intent of the word usage. In this same way, the exact same principle can be easily and scripturally applied to the Word of the Lord. Revelatory knowledge is much, much more than mere words upon a page or concepts to be memorized and recited through vain repetition. In fact, Jesus had much to say about the useless nature of vain repetition. "But when ye pray, use not vain repetitions as the heathens do: for they think that they shall be heard for their much speaking." (Matthew 6:7) Let's face it, so much of Christianity in today's world has become little more than a glamorized, overly-commercialized form of vain repetition – Sunday after Sunday filled with more of the same, still devoid of any miraculous power. However, I sense in you a great hunger for more. The very fact that you are now reading this book signifies your true intention. By studying and meditating upon the laws of God contained within this book and within the scriptures, your intention is revealing itself and making itself known: You want more.

You want to finally put into practice the great truth of the Spirit within your life and begin to attract the desires of your heart. Why does the religious mind cause us to be so fearful of success of abundance? We so often act as though prosperity, wealth, and abundance are bad things. The truth is how can we ever expect the world to take us seriously, when we speak of the blessings of the Lord, if we are not, in some way, reflecting the truth of abundance in our lives? Abundance and wealth go far beyond the materialistic sense and have very little to do with dollars and bank accounts. However, let me be perfectly clear. Money and finance serve a very powerful role within the life of the individual, and, no matter what lies religion has told you, God wants you to have more of it. "A feast is made for laughter, and wine maketh merry: but money answereth all things." (Ecclesiastes 10:19) The translation found within the New International Version says, quite frankly "Money is the answer to everything." Yes, as shocking as you may find that text, you read that correctly. Furthermore, Deuteronomy 8:18, says, "But thou shalt remember the Lord thy God: for it is he that giveth thee power to get wealth, that he may establish his covenant which he sware unto thy father, as it is this day." Notice the writer does not say that it is the Lord who gives wealth but, rather, it is the Lord who gives the *ability* to get wealth, in order to establish his covenant in the earth realm. In

pg. 50

other words, you recognizing your own ability to get wealth is so that the covenant – the universal principle of God – might be established for all to see. I will never apologize for the blessing of the Lord upon my life, and furthermore, I will never apologize for my ability to attract wealth. "The blessing of the Lord, it maketh rich, and he addeth no sorrow with it." (Proverbs 10:22)

Do you awaken each day sorrowfully? Do you literally feel a sense of dread each day, going into an environment which you absolutely despise? In order to work for someone else and make them rich, while you find yourself struggling to simply survive? This is not the covenant which the Lord established, my friend. The earthly system of the world now in play, which we see enacted literally all around us, is, quite literally, the antithesis – the opposite - of the covenant. However, it *is*, still, the principle of the "Law of Attraction" at work. Same thoughts and repetitive patterns create only more of the same. It really is true my friend. When you change your thoughts, you change your life. One of the most powerful passages within all of scripture, concerning the power of creative thought is found within the Book of Romans. "And be not conformed to this world: but be ye transformed by the renewing of your mind, that ye may prove what is that good, and acceptable, and perfect, will of God." (Romans

pg. 52

12:2) Hear me when I say to you that if it is not good to you, if it is not acceptable to you, and if it is not perfection for you, then it is *not* the perfect will of God being created in your life and something else is being created with your thoughts. Either way, the universe is at your command and has been the entire time, all along. Religious tradition *is* the enemy.

For centuries, we have allowed ourselves to be deceived into believing that if it happens within our lives then it must be the will of God. I mean, He controls everything, right? No, if it happens, then it is the creation of the mind of man. We so often have the erroneous belief that the will of God is always enacted. Nothing could be any more untrue. In fact, the will of God is very rarely enacted, fully, because of disagreement, disconnectedness, and a lack of unity within the minds of men. Either you are a conscious creator, or you are a careless creator. There is no in-between. Either way, you are a creator. In the very prominent and very popular "Word of Faith" movement within Pentecostal and Charismatic circles of Christianity, it isn't uncommon to find many sincere individuals holding up their Bibles and publicly declaring, "This is my Bible. I have what it says I have." As genuine and as sincerely well-intentioned as these brothers and sisters are, the blunt truth is that if they give their last one hundred dollars in the Sunday morning offering, only to drive home afterword fearful of running out of gas and being stranded on the roadside, only to return to a home in which an eviction notice has been left upon the door, they do *not* have what their Bibles say they have. I say that with all love and with all humility; however it is time that we begin to look beyond the lies of religion. Now, more than ever, it is time to awaken to the truth of the principles of God and cease to settle for elementary, childish, religious nonsense that builds megachurches yet leaves you in lack and in poverty. Something has to change, my friend, and that something is your own mindset and thinking.

God will never change. He simply *is*. "For I am the *Lord*, I change not; therefore ye sons of Jacob are not consumed." (Malachi 3:6) Your life will not change until you change it, my friend. You do this by beginning to create anew and afresh. This moment, as you read these words, perhaps, like countless millions of others throughout the world, you are now finding yourself literally struggling to simply make ends meet. Perhaps, like many, you find yourself simply losing hope, continually discouraged, because you do not see the manifestation of your promises. You are not here by accident. You are not here by happenstance. You did not simply come across this book because something triggered a curiosity within you. No, that something is the voice of the Spirit – your inner man. The real you. The inner Self knows what truth is. The inner Self always has and always will. The Christ in you is now stirring within as you read these words. I sense it. You now find yourself beginning to dream again – to hope again. You find yourself no longer content to simply survive and are now, finally, prepared to enter into a new revelatory season in which you begin to thrive. Are you ready to begin the journey? Are you ready to begin to paint upon a new, blank canvas, the dreams and visions which have consumed your heart? Today is the day that you can begin to walk into the full power and thrust of your own creative force. The

pg. 57

power of the Godhead – the Divine Mind which created all things and is still creating – lies within you, simply awaiting the instructions given by your own thoughts and decrees.

So often, I am asked by many, "Will it always be this way?" As you find yourself facing the daily struggle of lack and negativity and heartache, perhaps you now find yourself asking the exact same question? Will it always be this way?" "Will I always have to live like this?" The answer, my friend, is very simple. It does not have to be that way. You do not have to live *that* way.

GREATER DEPTHS

Within your innermost being, even within this very moment, there exists a certain restlessness. If you were to be honest with your own true Self, you would admit that it has been there for so very long – that yearning for more. When I say these things, I speak not of merely financial matters or of abundance in the materialistic sense. No, rather, I speak of a yearning for more of a sense of completion – a connectedness – a unity. In my younger life, when I first entered into the work of the ministry, sensing the call of God upon my life and feeling the pull of the prophetic towards people, I often found myself wondering, "What does this all mean?" In other words, what is it about the human experience that can only be truly satisfied by the spiritual truths of God? I began a journey in that season which I am even now continuing to walk and to explore – the scenery is always changing, as I find myself continuing to uncover even more and more revelatory knowledge. Even in studying the early works of the great Christian mystics and seers and visionaries, the founders of the church, I recognized that the hunger and the yearning existed from the very inception of the soul into human flesh. In the thirteenth century,

pg. 60

in the writing, *The Flowing Light of the Godhead*, Mechthild of Madgeburg wrote of man's connection with the Divine, "I can never be sundered from you. However far we parted, never can we be separated. I am in you and you are in me. We could not be any closer."

The psalmist said it in this way, "Whither shall I go from thy spirit? Or whither shall I flee from thy presence? If I ascend up into heaven, thou art there. If I make my bed in hell, behold, thou art there. If I take the wings of the morning, and dwell in the uttermost parts of the sea; even there shall thy hand lead me, and thy right hand shall hold me." (Psalm 139: 7-10) The hunger for the things of the Spirit is so ingrained and innate within all things. One cannot even fathom such a tremendous unity – such an interconnectedness which exists with mankind and the Divine. In those early days of my ministry, I so often felt the pull of the prophetic voice within and, at first, never knew what to call it. The terminology did little to define it, however, for it was simply the deep of God reaching out, calling out unto the deep within others. "Deep calleth unto deep at the noise of thy waterspouts: all thy waves and thy billows are gone over me." (Psalm 42:7) Many ask me, quite often, why I seem to place such an emphasis upon the power of the prophetic. Well, as a prophet called of God, it's truly all I've ever known – the prophetic voice has been

pg. 62

such an integral part of my daily life for as long as I can consciously remember. However, there is an even greater reason.

The prophetic voice places all things into alignment, again. "Surely the Lord GOD will do nothing, but he revealeth his secret unto his servants the prophets." (Amos 3:7) You see, my friend, you have a very real and tangible need for the prophetic within your own, daily life, whether you realize it, consciously, or not. I share much more about the essentiality of accessing the prophetic voice in my *School of the Prophets* course; however, according to the word of the Lord through the Prophet Amos, "The Lord God will do nothing, until his secrets are revealed to his servants the prophets." How can this be? Such a statement flies directly in the face of centuries of religious orthodoxy and Christian teaching which claim it is the Lord who does, well, practically everything for us. Not only is it essential to have the prophetic gift working and operating within your daily life, the truth of the matter is that it is actually very dangerous to attempt to live without it. Why? Well, because of the "Law of Attraction" always at work within our lives. Have you ever gone about your day, carefully and dutifully tending to your daily responsibilities when, all of the sudden and seemingly out of the blue, you find yourself feeling drawn to a certain thought or to images of certain things? To the point where it

pg. 64

seems as though it's almost next to impossible to get the images out of your mind? Or, rather, have you ever, in passing, encountered a complete and total stranger and had a sense of that person? Details about their life? Some would call this mere intuition or some form of psychic phenomena; however, the scriptures make it very plain this phenomena is, in fact, the prophetic voice. The imagery within your mind matters. Your thoughts matter. Concerning the "Law of Attraction," quite frankly, your thoughts literally matter – they become matter.

I share much more about this phenomenon in my teaching course, *School of Visualization*, available through Identity

Network; however, in summary, the imagery we see and visualize matters greatly. If thoughts truly do become things, as science has clearly proven, then not only are we at all times needing to remain ever-conscious and ever-vigilant of guarding our thoughts and what I call our "internal imagery," but we must remember that we are by our very nature powerful creators within the earth. "Keep thy heart (thoughts) with all diligence; for out of it are the issues of life." (Proverbs 4:23) In the 1984 film *Ghostbusters*, directed by Ivan Reitman, there is a very memorable scene near the ending of the film in which the stars are told that their thoughts would manifest and take shape and come to destroy them. Well, in an effort to

pg. 66

protect themselves, they quickly attempt to clear their minds, when, suddenly, the character portrayed by Dan Aykroyd accidentally and unintentionally envisions the Stay Puft Marshmallow Man. In the comical scene, almost instantaneously, a towering being made entirely out of marshmallow materializes and begins to attack the city. As hilarious as such a concept might seem, well, there is actually some very real and practical metaphysical truth woven and blended into the scene. Now, of course, I'm in no way attempting to suggest that we stand any real danger of ever being attacked by a creature made entirely out of marshmallow, but I simply mean that thought forms do materialize and, in some way, become things. It is a proven

pg. 67

scientific truth. Science and metaphysics are now beginning to finally recognize that the mysteries found within the Word of God are, in fact, very real and very true. In the realm of physics, there is an identified subatomic particle called the *Higgs boson.*

To put it quite simply, scientifically speaking, subatomic particles are truly what are responsible for giving properties to everything within the physical world. Some particles, such as protons, for instance, have a certain kind of mass on their own. Other particles, like photons, have absolutely no mass and are strictly made up of pure energy. Researchers and physicians believe the Higgs boson subatomic particle is the particle responsible for giving mass and weight and density to physical matter. Would you be curious to know what science has termed this mysterious subatomic particle? "The God Particle." To be fair to the researchers involved, the term "The God Particle" actually originated in a book by Leon Lederman, entitled, *The God Particle: If the Universe is the Answer, What is the Question?* The man who first proposed the existence of the Higgs boson particle, Peter Higgs, didn't originate the term. As I said earlier, however, terminology is of little importance. In fact, I often laugh, thinking to myself that scientists could have even termed the particle "Satan's Particle" and it would have made very little difference at all, because the truth is that the research proves what the Bible has been saying the entire time - there is a spiritual, energy component behind everything we see in the physical world. Science is proving the Word of God to be true. At the very core, most basic element of all things lies a very real spiritual energy and vibration. In other words, everything that we see in the three-dimensional, physical world is merely the result of small subatomic particles of pure spirit energy! The home you enjoy, although it may seem very tangible and physical, is nothing more than energy. The car you drive to work daily is made entirely of spiritual energy. The bank account and the money within it, although you can fold the paper bills and place your signature upon paper checks, it's all spiritual energy and nothing more.

This scientific research proves what I have prophetically known for years: literally everything we see is made up of a power we cannot see. Literally everything around us is, in fact, the power of the Spirit working and continuing to manifest. In a sense, the creation which began all those billions of years ago is still being enacted even now. Researchers confirm that the universe is, even at this very moment, continuing to expand. When creation began within the mind of God, it never ceased. It never stopped. It never ended. If anything, quantum physics teaches us that there is literally no detachment within the universe in any way. Sure, it may seem as though there is to the natural eyes and to the natural mind. It may appear as though there are multiple homes located on your street. It may seem, to the natural, five senses, that there is only a set amount of money within your bank account; however, there is only a singular, spiritual energy of creative force behind all of it. My friend, if you could receive this word then not only will it change your today, it will change your tomorrow, as well. The reason why the inner voice of the prophetic is so crucial and so integrally important to life is that it takes a prophetic and spiritual sensitivity to sense the

pg. 72

energy at work. It takes the prophetic sense to begin unlocking the patterns of old paradigms and to unleash the mind into a new revelatory way of thinking. This creative energy is the driving force behind the "Law of Attraction." It is literally the driving force, if you will, behind every visualization and all of the internal imagery being enacted onto the tapestry of the physical world we see each and every day. There is a sort of resonance at work, at all times, in all that we do and in all that we think.

With each and every image we reflect upon, we begin realigning the energy of our lives. Hear me, my friend, when I say to you, that the power of attraction is based entirely upon proper positioning and that the proper positioning begins with the state of your very own thinking and your belief system. Because of the fact that we are speaking of spiritual energy when dealing with the power of attraction, I must also say that there is a frequency at work, as well. There are so many who would even when first hearing the word "frequency," think, "That is such a 'new age' concept." My friend, these are those same individuals who have prayed for years about the new career, rather than stepping out on faith to begin the career they desire. These are those who have prayed for months for the Lord to send them the love life they have been imagining, rather than beginning to move out into a greater dimension of faith and confidence in order to actually meet the spiritual connection for them. Remember, as the Prophet Amos said, "The Lord GOD will do nothing" without having a prophetic voice in his servants. In other words, rather than sitting idly by and waiting for the Lord to act, right now, even today, begin to have an ear to hear what the Spirit is saying. Have a spiritual sensitivity to begin to see what the Lord is doing. Where is the energy moving within your life? Is it flowing forth, or is it stagnant and not moving at all? Today is the day to act. This is your prophetic word: "Move!" You know, when I begin to think of the term "frequency," I visualize a radio receiver. How often have we

pg. 75

needed to change the frequency in order to hear more clearly? In order to attract the signal much more freely and uninterrupted? Might I say to you, my friend, that the reason you have yet to attract the life you have truly wanted is because you have had your prophetic senses turned off and have been tuned into the wrong, lower frequency? Come up higher, into the deeper things of God – into the greater works and the deeper mysteries.

You see, although you are now, even in this moment, a very real byproduct of your own creative thoughts and although your present circumstances are in many ways byproducts of years of old patterns of behavior and old paradigms of thinking from seasons long expired, the beautiful thing about the power of creation is that although it is impossible to undo the creation process, it is absolutely possible to begin to recreate. For me, I so often find myself dreaming throughout the day. Quite often, I sit in my meditation garden, located on the grounds of my property, and just visualize the beauty of creation. As overly simplistic and as elementary as it might sound, an attitude of gratefulness goes a long way. In fact, the emotion of thankfulness and the feeling of gratitude is one of the elemental steps of releasing ourselves from the chains of our past creations. As I listen to the song of the birds and see the beautiful flowers blossoming, I am reminded of just how

pg. 77

incredibly creative the power of the Spirit truly is. If you truly want to experience the essence of God, simply take a moment to enjoy nature. Find time to get out and partake in the beauty of the day, even if just for a moment. I promise you will be quite surprised to feel the worries and cares of life begin to vanish as you simply take time each day to recognize mindfulness. To think that the beauty of this world existed in the mind and heart of a loving creator for no other reason than his own good pleasure and his own desire to create, it's a reminder to us that we possess the same creative power. When you begin to take time each day to become awakened and aware to even the simply joys – time with friends, the beauty of nature, the

pg. 78

sound of your favorite song – I promise you will begin to feel an inner sense of inspiration growing within you. Find an inspiration that is unique to you. Whether you find it in art, in music, in time with friends, or, quite simply, in times of meditation, take time to be inspired each day.

The word "inspiration," in fact, is a reminder to be "in-spirited." In those moments of inspiration, we begin to be reminded by the creative voice within. We re-member and come back to the place of unity, within ourselves and with the world around us. Never before has there been such a need to go after a much more in-spirited life. You may be saying, "Jeremy, I work so much that I rarely even have a moment to myself." I understand, believe me. In fact, with my touring schedule for ministry, I know, firsthand, just how overwhelming it can seem to balance time. Sometimes it can seem as though there just aren't enough hours in a day to be as productive and creative as we would like to be. However, there is always tomorrow, thankfully. If you, like so many others, are, perhaps, feeling as if you can never find enough time in the day to re-center, re-focus, and to re-align and re-member, may I respectfully ask, what are you doing with your time? What are you doing where you are, in the time you do have? Why not use it to begin to dream. Begin to visualize. Begin envisioning the life you truly want, in

pg. 80

spite of the current circumstances of the creation you now find yourself living within. Begin to recreate by setting a new decree within your heart. Begin allowing the internal imagery – your visualization – to draft the plans for the life you are about to manifest. Think about the dream. Study it carefully within your mind. Daydream more. By beginning to shift your focus even ten to fifteen minutes a day toward the life you wish to create, you will be amazed at just how easily you will begin to make it a part of your daily practice. Besides, in all honesty, it just feels good to envision the life you truly want. I promise you, my friend, by beginning to adopt these moments of visualization into your daily life, very soon you will actually feel your inner man beginning to awaken.

Every manifestation first began with an inner vision, without exception. Every book I have written began, first, with a dream. My travels around the globe took place, first, within my mind's eye, long before ever stepping foot aboard a plane. The conferences which I have been privileged to minister at – often to audiences of tens of thousands of individuals – they began, first, within an inner dream. I kept the vision and the dream within my heart, meditating upon it daily – studying upon it – until the books were manifested, the air miles logged and the sermons preached. I want to encourage you to begin dreaming again. When Joseph found himself ostracized, persecuted, and abandoned by family, he began to dream another dream. As he continued to dream, he soon found himself in the palace of the king, a ruler over all the land. I will share more regarding the power of the dream soon; however, in this moment allow me to simply remind you to begin to dream anew. Begin to dream a brand new dream for your life. Envision the home you truly desire, the relationship you have craved, and the career you have always wanted. With each thought and with each moment of visualization, not only are you beginning to place the artist's brush upon the canvas, you are beginning to complete a masterpiece within the world of the Spirit. When the masterpiece is completed there, within the realm of the Spirit – in the mind – it will have no choice but to manifest into the three-dimensional world around you.

The laws of God are never broken. They are Divine in every way and are built upon universal principles, like the law of gravity here within our world. When the masterpiece is completed and the spiritual energy is aligned and remembered, the universe has no choice but to respond. Remember, the entire universe is at your command. All of Heaven is at your beck and   call.

IDENTITY OF ATTRACTION

In the days following the ascension of Jesus, it was a time a great persecution. There had been so many miracles. The miraculous had become the norm, in any regards. Then, all those who had once so happily walked away from everything in order to follow him were all of the sudden finding themselves alone, in hiding, in an upper room. His final instructions to them before being taken from their midst was to tarry in the city of Jerusalem – to wait – until they would be endued with power from on high.

What had it all meant? I often wonder what must have been within the minds of those first disciples as they gathered there that day. On the crowded and busy streets below visitors filled the streets, in Jerusalem to celebrate the Jewish feast of Pentecost. And suddenly, everything changed. In an instant, questions were answered. It all became so clearly apparent the road that was to be walked. Pentecost, that defining moment in the birth of the church can be summarized in one word: unity. They were there, in one accord – together. That which was within began to be manifested without, and all of Jerusalem saw it and heard it. Awakening had come, as the mighty God in Christ, clothed in flames of fire, became the Christ in them. A ragamuffin band of misfits and outcasts had, in a moment of supernatural overflow been reborn into a great and a mighty army. Peter – who had only days before publicly denounced Jesus for fear of his own life – stood boldly and declared the mysteries of God, proudly for all to hear.

The concept of identity is such a vital part of the process of manifestation, particularly when dealing with the power of creative force. A Divine union had been enacted. In the flames of Pentecost, each individual had become forged to the other, leaving behind any semblance of separation of disconnectedness. If you were to study the Book of Acts, you would find that because of this new identity, the miraculous was manifested daily within the lives of the Apostles. Now, more than two millennia later, we find ourselves at a crossroads, yet again, and the Spirt is reminding the whole of humanity to awaken to its true identity and assume its identity as creator. "Before I formed thee in the belly I knew thee; and before thou camest forth out of the womb I sanctified thee a prophet unto the nations." (Jeremiah 1:5) These words of the Lord, spoken through the Prophet Jeremiah give us a glimpse, yet again, of the role that we are to play within the earth realm – the role of a Divine voice.

Before Pentecost drew night, Jesus had commanded his followers to wait for the promise of power, and he had done so for a very specific reason. "But yet shall receive power, after that the Holy Ghost is come upon you: and ye shall be witnesses unto me both in Jerusalem, and in all Judea, and in Samaria, and unto the uttermost part of the earth." (Acts 1:8) Not only had the Divine fire sparked within them the revelatory knowledge of their true identity, it had also equipped them for a very specific purpose: to be a witness within the earth realm. You see, to create and manifest miraculously, one must first, above all else, recognize that they truly possess the power and the ability to do so. Secondly, he or she must put their innate power into practice in order to change their world. Today, in this moment, you possess within you a power to change your world – not only the entirety of the globe, but, most importantly, your own personal sphere of influence. Let's make it personal, shall we?

You possess the power to create opportunities for advancement and to create the life you have truly been destined to live. By not utilizing your power for that purpose, you are not only wasting the power which you truly possess, but you are failing to establish the Kingdom of God within the earth. What if I told you that unless you begin attracting and creating the life you desire – utilizing the law of creation to begin creating and attracting consciously – that the Kingdom of God will never truly be established? It's true, really. Not only is it your Divine birthright to create, but it is also your responsibility and purpose to do so. The entire world is looking to see a demonstration of the creative power of God within the earth, and it will not until you begin to create more effectively than you have. I say that not to condemn or to cast blame but, rather, to encourage and to edify.

You have unlimited resources at your disposal, even as you are reading these words. In fact, these resources have always existed around you, whether you have ever been consciously aware of it or not. You may think, "Jeremy, you haven't seen my bank account and all of the expenses I have; how can you possibly say that I have unlimited resources?" I say this because I know your true identity, even if, for the moment, you may have forgotten who you are. I know who you *truly* are. I see the Christ in you. I see you as the creator you are. Allow me to explain. As I shared with you earlier, the idea of separation and disconnectedness is merely a religious concept, based entirely in misguided and misplaced judgment. The Divine pattern of God is one of unity, utter Oneness, and collectiveness. Now, when I speak of the topic of Oneness, I'm not necessarily referring to the concept within Christology known as modalism or a rejection of a triune nature. The oneness I speak of far, far supersedes any man-

pg. 92

made interpretation of theology of religious dogma. I'm referring not to the oneness within the Godhead – the union of the Son with the Father – rather, I'm speaking of the Oneness which we, as believers share within the Godhead. Just as Jesus is, so are we. Now, I know that for generations we've been indoctrinated to believe we are separate from God and nothing more than depraved, sinful humans – capable of very little, other than sin. Stop believing these lies about yourself. In fact, the sooner you can begin to see yourself in perfect union with God - because of Christ - the sooner you will stop believing that you are undeserving of the abundance and unlimited resource the universe is waiting to give you.

pg. 93

I know that in your present circumstance and current surroundings it may seem as if you have been waiting patiently and faithfully for God to bless you, but I swear to you that is simply not the case. You are not waiting on the universe; the universe is waiting on you. One of the most erroneous and damnable concepts of religion is the concept of "waiting of God." I in no way seem to suggest that there aren't certain periods of preparation that exist within our life paths; however, even in those seasons there are laws of creation and attraction being enacted in each moment of time. In other words, even in the waiting, there is work being done. This erroneous religious lie is the reason why many have gone to the grave without ever fully

pg. 94

manifesting the creative power lying within them to change their own lives through the power of manifestation. Today, unfortunately, there are many sincere believers – genuine and authentic men and women of the faith – who have seemingly, heartbreakingly lost ten, twenty, and thirty years of time waiting for God to change their circumstances and surroundings, rather than beginning to unlock their own creative power and master their own worlds of creation.

Today, in this religious culture of lies we now find ourselves living within, many believers pray for two or three years about whether or not they should even begin a home

Bible study group or join the choir. In the Book of Acts, when the early followers became infused with their own creative identity, this simply was not the case. There was no wasted time; there was only the law of creation being enacted to manifest the miraculous. One of my favorite passages of scripture detailing this fact is actually rarely spoken of from behind most pulpits; however, prophetically speaking, I believe this passage of scripture details explicitly the Divine partnership of creation within our union within the Godhead. In studying the Book of Acts, if most aren't careful they will entirely miss this principle. This passage is found in Acts 15:28. "For it seemed good to the Holy Ghost, and to us, to lay upon you no greater burden then these necessary things." I want you to pay particularly close attention to the words, "and to us." Therein lies one of the most profound concepts of the miraculous power of creation found within the early church – the concept of perfect partnership and union. You see, my friend, so often we attempt to sit idly by, waiting for the Holy Ghost to enact some miracle or sign or wonder – some manifestation – when the entire time there is a role that we must play, in order to enact the power of creation and attraction. You may think that your present circumstances seem good to the Holy Ghost, but I want to ask you, does your life seem good to *you*? If not, then you are not in partnership and you are out of creative alignment.

As the Spirit of God awakened the minds of the early believers, they became emboldened to create. This illustrates the truth of the power of attraction in a very transcendent way. "And they went forth, and preached everywhere, the Lord working with them, and confirming the word with signs following. Amen." (Mark 16:20) This supernatural partnership of co-creation and of perfect union with the Godhead is an example of the force of creation we begin to access as we are freed from old paradigms of thinking and begin viewing ourselves as creators in the earth realm. The term "Lord" in the passage of Mark 16:20 is the term "kurio" in Greek, meaning "authority." The Hebrew term of the same meaning, again, would be "Elohim," translated as "judge." Again, I ask you, my friend, when you judge the life you now find yourself living, does it seem good to you? If not, don't you think it's time you begin the step into your true identity as creator within your life? In my teaching course, *Connecting to Creation Resources*, from my *School of Visualization* series, I share very detailed steps which outline these truths in even greater depth. If we are "in" God, as scripture repeatedly bears out within, both, the Old and New covenants, and if, as Amos said, "The Lord will do nothing" without the prophetic

pg. 99

anointing, then don't you think it's time you become freed from the religious mind of bondage and lack once and for all? Religion promotes detachment, isolationism, and a mindset of poverty and lack, not because believers aren't sincere in their faith and well-intentioned in their beliefs but because the system of beliefs is built upon the faulty premise that we are disconnected from creative power. You are the Lord within the earth, as much as it pains the religious mind to accept it. "Neither shall they say, Lo here! or, lo there! for, behold, the kingdom of God is within you." (Luke 17:21) The earthly ministry of Jesus was always one of unity, not of disconnectedness. Not only did he embody perfectly the oneness

pg. 100

with the Father, but he, in turn shared the truth of our oneness within the Godhead, also. While in the garden, the prayer of Jesus to the Father depicts this truth best. "And the glory which thou gavest me I have given them; that they may be one, even as we are one." (John 17:22) My friend, it cannot be shared any more plainly: *You* are the Lord within the earth and within your sphere of daily living, and *you* are the creator within your own life.

There is no creative force which exists outside of you which is not also permeating you at all times. The early disciples recognized this and manifested the "Law of Attraction" daily. The prophetic voice is a voice of identity. There is a reason my work is called Identity Network. Everything your Bible says about Jesus applies to you, and because of his oneness with the Godhead, that means everything the Bible says about the Godhead it also says about you. Yes, you read that correctly. Again, I say that not only is it your birthright to be a creator but it is your responsibility to create and attract the life you truly want to live in this earth, so that the glory of God might be made manifested within the earth. Religion is nothing more than a cult ideology, meant to separate us from the truth of who we have always been. Have you ever wondered why most who kidnap or who abuse prefer to keep their victims in places of isolation, separated from others? Why they

pg. 102

keep them in places of darkness? It's simply because it gives them the ability to control and to indoctrinate and to manipulate. There is power in unity. You identity is one of unity. You are, even now, connected to all things and all things are connected to you – there is absolutely nothing apart from you, even now in this given moment. The blessing you want is already connected to you.

The miracle you have been in need of is already connected to you. In reality, because of your identity as creator you truly have need of nothing. May I share with you a truth that will completely revolutionize your way of thinking? Lack is merely an illusion. It in no way truly exists within the universe. The idea of lack is simply a mindset, based upon current perception. Thankfully, with a prophetic word of truth, a perception can change and a perspective is able to be shifted. Did you know that energy attracts energy? Like truly does attract like. Job said that which he had feared the most had come upon him, meaning that the focus of our thoughts truly does have creative power to manifest. The object of your focus is the life you now live. I can always tell what the object of an individual's focus truly is. In fact, it doesn't even require the gift of prophecy to be able to recognize it. Do you want to see what someone's object of focus truly is? Simply look at their outward life. Thoughts of lack attract lack and thoughts of abundance attract more abundance. There is absolutely no escaping it, regardless of your beliefs. As I shared earlier, there is an energy and a frequency behind all things in the material, physical world. The word "energy" is derived from the root term "energeia," meaning "productive work." This root term is used in the original language of scripture a total of eight times, throughout, and in the New Testament it is used to denote not only the work of "production" but also "superhuman strength." Interestingly, on one such occasion, the term is used when Moses asked to see the visible glory of God atop the mountain. If the account were to be read in the original language, the Lord quite literally responds by saying that He would allow his "energy" to pass before the face of Moses. My friend, energy is the very nature of God – and of you – in "productive action." Being that all of creation exists with a certain energy vibration and frequency, it is always subject to change. The changing or the "bending" of energy is not merely some mystical or metaphysical concept; it is entirely scriptural and based absolutely within the creative power which we possess as believers, through the inner Christ within.

When the Apostle Peter encountered the lame man and commanded him to rise up and walk, there was a literal "bending" of the energy at play which not only caused strength to enter

pg. 106

into the legs of the lame man but also caused a shifting within the mind which resulted in him being able to be healed. In other words, scientifically speaking, the "God Particle" was at work and responding to the sound of Peter's voice, thoughts, and command. In that miraculous moment of healing, the entire universe was subject to the voice, thoughts, and commands of the Apostle. In that moment, Peter was using the power of his own creative force. You see, my friend, we must settle the issue within our minds once and for all that the will of God is being enacted in cooperation with our will – there are no longer two wills, but one singular will. Long gone are the days in which we must strive to pray for the will of God within

pg. 107

our lives. Christ changed all of that by causing us to possess the ability to be regenerated through our thoughts, the moment that we became endued with the power of the Spirit within. Now, there is working within you a great and powerful "energeia," or "energy" of creative power which has placed you into alignment with all of the energy contained within the Godhead and within the physical universe. Now, when I say to my students and to audiences around the world that their identity is that of the Godhead, I don't say that as some religious euphemism or as some inspirational mantra. No, my friend, I mean it quite literally, indeed.

There exists around you at all times unlimited resource and abundance, and as you will soon begin to see and recognize, the only thing which is limiting you is actually you, yourself – through your mind and your thoughts. In this revolutionary teaching, you are even now discovering who you are – your true and most authentic identity. You are not merely a sinner saved by the grace of God. Now, because of the work of the inner Christ and all that was accomplished upon the cross, you are even now the very living, physical embodiment of the Godhead within the earth realm. You are a powerful speaking and thinking spirit, here to declare the glory of God within the earth. It's beyond time that you recognize who you truly

pg. 109

are so that you can begin to create the life you truly desire. If you now find yourself unhappy with the life you've created and if it doesn't "seem good" to you, then it's time to begin to recreate. It's time to begin to mold and to bend the "energeia" at will, for the purposes of your own good pleasure and will. When God looked out upon the firmament and into the terrestrial plane of earth to gaze upon his creation, He said His creation was "good." It literally felt good to Him to see what He had accomplished. Today, the universe is simply awaiting your command in order to come into alignment with your decree and the command you send out with your thoughts. Are you ready to truly be the master of the universe, as God intended? If so, you can

begin   the   journey   today.

MYSTERIES OF THE MIND

"For who hath known the mind of the Lord, that we may instruct him? But we have the mind of Christ." (1 Corinthians 2:16)

It is impossible to speak of the attractive, creative power of the mind and not also speak of the importance of memory. Concerning the memory, I know, quite often, the very idea of memories can sometimes feel like much more of a curse rather than a blessing. In fact, if we were to be completely honest with ourselves, there are often times so many instances that we'd just as soon choose to forget. The painful moments. The tragic accident. The moment we said goodbye to the love of our lives who had once promised to always stand by our side – the moment we watched them walk away from us for the very last time. Memories – the mental pictures within our mind – is so much more than just the historic score from a legendary Broadway musical. Memories are Divine in nature. In fact, they not only serve a very real purpose and a very important place within our spiritual awakening, but they also are a powerful blessing and not a curse or some heavy burden the universe is asking us to continue to bear.

pg. 114

Memories, quite simply put, remind us that we've moved forward. That we've been through something. That we have a story to share. Memories remind us of the emotional scars we have acquired, always beckoning us to remember the most pivotally transitional aspects of our journeys.

Quite literally, our memories are markers of our mile stones, the universal gauge of just how very far we have already come. As with all things in life, Divine perspective is everything. I was speaking with a woman once who had been directed to me for a life coaching session for business. She was in the midst of preparation to take a major step of faith and launch out into the deep waters by starting her very own business. In fact, it was questions regarding her business that had drawn her to me. She had come to inquire of the Lord a prophetic word to give her a glimpse of what the upcoming season would hold. "Will it be a success?" "How long before I begin to yield a return on my investment?" "Will people enjoy my services?" All of these questions came forth like a rushing river from a woman who seemed to have so very much going for her. To most who encountered her in passing, it seemed as though she was on top of the world with everything in her favor. And then the tears began to flow. Like a flood gate of the soul being opened, her true heart began to pour forth from within her. "I'm so sorry," she exclaimed." "I wasn't expecting to get so emotional." Having been in ministry for most of my life, I am well acquainted of the human body's reaction to the glory and the presence of God; however, this was something else altogether. It was a spiritual purging – so beautiful to behold, really. As I saw the tears streaming down her face, her mascara beginning to run, I knew I was beholding the sensitive mind of a fellow creator at work. "After my husband left and abandoned me and the kids and left us for a younger woman, I just knew I had to take my power back. I had to start over again. I went back to school and that's what inspired me to launch the new business." I felt

pg. 117

the presence of God, as I heard her speak. As she spoke, the tears continued to flow. She was remembering, and I felt so very privileged to be a part of her journey for just a brief moment.

Then, there was Anthony, a young man who had attended one of my workshops in New York while I was on a book tour several years ago. I can still see his face so very vividly in my mind's eye. "Please remember me when you pray," he humbly asked. I felt the pain in his words. His pain pierced my soul, in fact. I sensed by the Spirit the cause of the pain. "When I was eleven years old, I was molested by my uncle," he shared, with tears streaming down his face. "I'm thirty now, and I feel like

I've never really known how to accept love in my life." So much of his adult life had been consumed by a memory that no one should ever have to endure. His memories were in the process of becoming a very powerful testimony of overcoming power. In fact, the testimony is how we overcome anything, really. We can be healed. We can be delivered. We can begin to overcome. However, the memories remain. And for what purpose? To what extent does memory serve us? Knowing that we have the very mind of God is to know that we, too, also have the Divine memory of God – the entirety of the Divine Mind working in us and through us. Even as we forgive and accept, the memories remain. Biologically, physiologically speaking, even the physical brain the human form possesses while within the earth realm, here, is, in itself, a testament to the mysteries and patterns of God. The scriptures are replete with illustrations and coded mysteries revealing very specific cycles and patters. The use of numbers throughout scripture is an example of this. One very Divine number is the number three. Jesus rose physically from the grave upon the third day. The incarnation into human flesh – into our nature within the earth – reveals a spirit, a soul, and a body. The tabernacles of scripture contained three very distinct and separate aspects: an outer court, and inner court, and the most holy place, which contained the ark of God. The number three is very

pg. 120

significant, obviously. "And if one prevail against him, two shall withstand him; and a threefold cord is not quickly broken." (Ecclesiastes 4:12) The number three represents the power of connection.

According to Jewish custom, once something was done three times, it was considered a very permanent thing, referred to as a "chazakah." According to Jewish mystics, once something is done three times, the individual connects to it and brings in into this world. The human brain consists of three parts, each working together to accomplish a very specific, overall task. However, each aspect of the brain performs individual tasks. Did you know that, in truth, you actually have three brains? The first brain, often called the Reptilian brain by some, is the portion of the brain made of the brain stem and the cerebellum. The second brain is composed of the limbic system, and the third brain is referred to as the "neocortex," or the "thinking" brain. A recent study by researchers at MIT suggested that long-term memories are stored indefinitely within the neocortex. The neocortex is also the aspect of the brain responsible for what we would refer to as "cognitive" functioning, like paying attention to detail or being able to think ahead in detailed ways and make plans. In others words, your creative power and your ability to think is a very detailed and very intricate process of inner workings within your brain.

You were created to remember. You were created to think. You were created to plan ahead and to dream and to cast vision for your life. The truth is, you were never designed to escape the memory of certain events or certain circumstances which you have endured – even the most painful of moments is meant to be remembered. These memories are so very important and integral to your decision to begin to create a new life for yourself. In other words, the trauma, regardless of how very unfair and wrong it was, created a memory within a moment of time, and it is within that memory of the trauma that you are now able to gauge your present and future life much differently. "I'm never going back to that." "I want a different life." I'm overcoming." "I'm moving forward." "I'm going to attract the love life I deserve." My friend, all of these decisions could not be made without a memory of the past. The memory is the reminder that you have endured something – that you've been somewhere before. It is the very foundational basis for your testimony, and, because of this, it is paramount to your process of future creation and attraction. Unfortunately, so very often, many find themselves stuck in old paradigms of the mind – old wiring, as I like to call it. Those who are familiar with refurbishing investment properties know that the interior – the behind the scenes – is often even more important than the exterior of a home. Do you know how many home fires are caused within the United States each day simply because of faulty wiring and old, out-of-date circuitry? Faulty, old wiring can not only be quite a very real inconvenience, but it can also be quite literally extremely dangerous. So it is with the wiring within the mind. Thankfully, however, the brain can be successfully rewired and old, out of date paradigms can be brought up to date.

I'm sure you're familiar with the phrase "Snap out of it," that's often said to those who we feel need a drastic shift in thinking. Well, believe it or not, there's actually a very real truth behind the phrase. You see, at all times, even though we aren't aware of it, all throughout the day and night, there are continuous "snaps" and "pops" happening inside the brain. At all times, a very real and powerful electromagnetic current is flowing throughout the brain, and, with each firing of the synapses, recognition is taking place. This is why someone in a comatose state is pronounced clinically dead when all brain activity ceases to function, although, outwardly, the function of breathing may be continued through the assistance of a ventilator. In other words, the powerful electromagnetic energies of the brain are constantly at work, at all times. The very

pg. 126

fact that you are now reading these words is proof-positive that you are conscious, alert, and still retain your cognitive function. You're able to understand and to process feeling and thought. Reading these words now, so much is happening behind the scenes. This is why the concept of memories is so vitally important and why the power of using our energy to create is so very dependent upon the functioning or the inner mind. If you don't know where you've been, how can you possibly decide where you'd like to go? How can you possibly recognize what you want to feel if you haven't, in some way, experienced traumatic moments which you would never wish to face again? This is the very real and Divine power of the testimony.

pg. 127

My friend, even now as you are processing these words, your brain is quite literally being rewired and a new form of circuitry is being created – literally, speaking. There is a very real scientific concept often referred to as "neural plasticity." Science continues to prove that the brain is being remolded, reshaped, and reformed each and every day, through our many, many unique and diverse experiences. As staggering as the figure may seem to the natural mind, the human brain is made up of more than 100 billion neurons, which make more than 100 trillion neural connections at any given moment. According to Michael Merzenich, in his book *The Brain That Changes Itself*, new habits are always being

pg. 128

formed, as a result of these "pathways." Let's look at this in a very practical way, in very practical terms. When you encounter a feeling or a thought or an event which causes you to begin to feel happy, in those moments, the brain is literally being rewired and literally strengthening the inner "pathways" making it much easier to begin to feel a greater sense of happiness more intensely and even more frequently. Are you beginning to finally understand now the very real creative power of the mind and why it is so vital that you begin your rewiring process right now? My friend, your memories, will always and forever remain, just as they were intended to. However, you have the creative power even now in this very moment to either dwell in the place of the past of to begin to advance into a greater dream. Either way, regardless of your choice, your thoughts are creating and shaping your reality, no matter what choice you make.

Memories are very important, also, because they assist in helping us gauge future decisions and planning. I would never dare suggest that there aren't very real victims of traumatic circumstances; there are. However, victimhood is only a temporary moment of time and God never designed you to dwell there. There have been some very painful moments within your life. Many of these moments were caused by your own doing and many were not;

however, I encourage you to refuse to live on those moments. You are not defined by singular moments of time and singular traumatic moments. I prophesy to you in this moment that you would, even now, begin to recognize and remember the power of your creative force. Remember that, even now, the universe is working to align and position itself around you in the way that you are commanding it to, for your reality. Whether you realize it or not, you have always been commanding the universe to answer your decrees. The problem has been, quite simply, that you haven't been awakened to the conscious awareness of it – the truth of the behind the scenes being enacted all around you. Well, now, today, there are no more excuses.

pg. 131

Regardless of where you've been and regardless of the trauma you've faced, this moment is the beginning of a new creation being enacted. Oh, if you could begin to embrace this truth of creation, you will never again be the same from this moment on. Right now, even as you read these words and begin to embrace this truth, your brain is being literally molded, reshaped, and reformed in order for you to absorb the feeling which you now are dwelling upon. Where is the focus? Is it upon the past or is it upon a greater dream of the life you wish to possess? Whatever the focus and the intention is right now is what your brain is being molded and literally shaped and sculpted to enforce.

Although, at first glance, brains may seem very similar in nature and they may contain many of the same, basic, physical properties, the truth is that no two brains are alike in any way. Just as finger prints are unique to the individual, so, too, is the brain unique to the individual. Why? Because the experiences of no two individuals are ever truly identical, in any way. I promise if you were to take an extended vacation with your significant other or, for that matter, even with a child, upon returning home you would remember the trip much, much differently than the others with you. Perhaps you enjoy long drives and travel by plane and they don't. Perhaps you were so very pleased with the delicious meal you ordered at the restaurant and, maybe their entrée wasn't prepared to their liking. Maybe, just maybe, you enjoyed the drive because you love to always view the passing, ever-changing scenery and they chose to sleep the entire way. Whatever the circumstances were, although you shared the exact same trip to the exact same destination at the exact same time, your experiences were not their experiences because they processed the information differently. You've asked why some are truly successful and seem to possess the "Midas Touch," while other, many well-intentioned and sincere individuals are living paycheck to paycheck and struggling daily, simply to survive. Well, this is the reason. The mindsets are different. The thinking is different. The thoughts and the behaviors have created different outcomes and experiences, based entirely upon the focal point of the intention.

The rich man and the poor man are, both, masters and creators, my friend. The only difference is that the poor man has been creating with misguided and misplaced thoughts. Do you realize, now, just how important the mind is within the creative process? How, whether we like it or not, our physical brains have always been formed to our very specific thoughts? You see, when I say to audiences around the world that the universe is at their command, I don't say that as merely some spiritual cliché. No, I mean it quite literally, in fact. When asked the secret of my success all these years, well, this is it. I realized very early on that I am the creator of my own life experiences and manifestations. This creative power which lies continually at our disposal is the very nature and glory of God. As an extension of Source energy within the earth realm, I am continually gauging, day by day, the thoughts which flow through my mind, always asking if it seems "good." If the answer is no, then I simply change my focus as quickly as possible because I know, full well, that extended focus and prolonged meditation upon a specific idea or thought form quickly causes a new neural pathway to be formed.

pg. 136

Is it always easy to guard the heart? Absolutely not. Often times it requires great persistence and focus. Above all, it requires being consistent, day by day. Positivity is not simply a spiritual exercise to be put to use in certain moments. No, it is a daily way of life that can only come through repeated practice. Daily, I set my intended focus, like placing sights upon the intended target. After a while, the intended target is reached. This principle works 100 percent of the time, without fail. Whether you find yourself just now beginning to be more conscientious of your creative power or whether you've been making it a point to live consciously awakened for years, just as I have, we are all in this journey together. The power within me is the power within you, and that power is the innate power of creation. Far too often, we use the memory of the past as a heavy and burdensome weight of baggage, rather than as the catalyst of change and fuel to prompt a recreation of our lives. Today, regardless of what you have endured or experienced, you are, even now, beginning to realize that you have always had a very real say in the matter.

Today, I want you to begin to view the experiences of the past as simply catalysts by which to gauge – or to "judge" – the current and present situation of your life. Begin to take account of your own actions and your own ways of thinking – the patterns of thoughts forms within your mind which have in a very real way led you to your current surroundings. The Spirit within is the voice of truth. Remember, my friend, the Spirit leads us into all truth – not partial truth – and the genuine *truth* of the matter is that you now have an opportunity to be a much more conscientious creator, rather than a careless creator. Perhaps, you have been so very flippant and very careless and irresponsible with your thoughts and intent and words in times past. We've all, at some point, been where you are. However, today is a day of awakening for you. According to Psalm 127:1, "Except the Lord build the house, they labor in vain that build it." As difficult as it is, at times, for us to take responsibility for our own

pg. 139

creation, the truth is that for much of your life, you have been working to build a house with old and out-of-date wiring. Today is a day filled with countless opportunities to rewire the old wiring, behind the scenes – it's a day to begin to recreate. You can begin to reprogram the old circuitry to become much, much more effective.

Consider today, this moment of awakening and recognition, as the time when the inspector of the universe – the Spirit – has served you with a notice of noncompliance, demanding that you update the inner wiring of the home you now reside in. As I've said before, the body is merely a temporary place of residence. The real you – the soul of you – is the inner man, which is being renewed day by

day   and   moment   by   moment.

pg. 142

THE CONSCIOUS

CREATION

I realized very early on, even in my young, early life before entering ministry, that there is no such thing as luck. The idea of luck is merely a man-made concept and idea. In truth, the idea of luck is far too often the excuse of laziness. Many so often look to those who have attained a great degree of success and say to themselves, "They must have gotten a lucky break in life." The very idea of luck is not only an idea steeped in laziness, but it is entirely

pg. 143

dismissive and disrespectful of the power of creation which we, all possess within the earth realm. According to 2 Chronicles 1:10, King Solomon asked of the Lord, "Give me wisdom and knowledge, that I may lead this people, for who is able to govern this great people of yours." According to tradition, when speaking in terms of success, many so often refer to King Solomon as the richest man who ever lived. According to the Hebrew Bible, it was during the reign of King Solomon that Israel gained its highest amount of wealth and splendor. A glimpse of the wealth of Solomon is given to us in 2 Chronicles 9:13-29, revealing that wealth was quite literally brought to him from all throughout the known world. The passage

pg. 144

begins by revealing that each and every year, Solomon was brought more than twenty-five tons of gold, in addition to the taxes being paid into the land. "And King Solomon passed all the kings of the earth in riches and wisdom. And all the kings of the earth sought the presence of Solomon , to hear his wisdom, that God had put in his heart. And they brought every man his present, vessels of silver, and vessels of gold, and raiment, harness, and spices, horses, and mules, a rate year by year." (2 Chronicles 9: 22-24)

Isn't it interesting to note that the most successful, most wealthy man who ever lived, because of his knowledge and thoughts, was not only given the ability to attain and build wealth but was also given the creative power to *attract* wealth? Other kings from all throughout the known world came to him and literally paid him for his vast knowledge? This passage of scripture defines the power of the law of attraction at work, perhaps more than any other passages within scripture. "If any of you lack wisdom, let him ask of God, that given to all men liberally and upbraideth not; and it shall be given him." (James 1:5) According to scripture, unlimited knowledge has always been at our disposal, simply awaiting the asking and the receiving. Knowing this, how can we in good conscious have the audacity to say that the wealth and success of some is merely a matter of luck? How can we even have the gall to make such claims when the scriptures clearly bear out that the knowledge to attain and attract such wealth is freely give to all men, liberally, if we would only ask for such knowledge? You see, my friend, not only is success and abundance not a matter of luck, as some would like to claim – a mere rolling of the dice, so to speak – it is based upon a very divine principle of creative power. You do not have because you do not ask.

According to James 4:2, "Ye lust and have not; ye kill, and desire to have, and cannot obtain; ye fight and war, yet ye have not, because ye ask not." The New International

Version translation states it in this way: "You desire but do not have, so you kill. You covet but you cannot get what you want, so you quarrel and fight. You do not have because you do not ask God." These scriptures bear out explicitly that rather than wasting valuable time coveting what others have built or have or have created that we must simply ask for our own ability to attain and to attract. My friend, it is simply the knowledge that must be asked for. How often, instead, have we seen and heard so many sincere individuals asking for the car or the increase in finances or the new home, rather than asking for the knowledge to attain and attract wealth? Do you realize that, although we speak of Solomon as the richest man who ever

pg. 148

lived, not once in the entirety of scripture do we ever find an account of him asking for his wealth? Think about that. Not once did Solomon ask the Lord for the gold and the riches and the position of influence and power. No, rather he asked, simply for wisdom and knowledge.

My friend, for millennia, humanity has been going about it all wrong, simply because it has not awakened to the power of the mind and the laws of creation and attraction. As I've said, the rich man and the poor man, both, possess the same abilities and creative faculties; the difference lies solely within the perception of the intended target of focus. It is the Lord who gives liberally and freely, not the wealth but knowledge to attain and to attract wealth. When first launching out in public ministry all those years ago, I began to ask the Lord for prophetic insight and revelatory knowledge. Never in my wildest dreams at the time would I have ever even imagined being able to deliver the Word of the Lord to celebrities, governors, and heads of state from across the globe. I didn't ask for the opportunity; I asked for the revelatory knowledge. It was the knowledge which made the difference. My friend, each and every month, requests pour into Identity Network from throughout the world, from heads of state and those in positions of prominence as heads of business, reaching out to simply ask for a

pg. 150

prophetic word. I have counseled literally millions from throughout the world through these engagements and also through my various travels and conferences all these years. Concerning speaking engagements, people often find it unbelievable when I say that not once in more than thirty years of ministry have I ever had the need to contact a church or conference host or venue and ask if I could be added as a speaker. Not even once. Not once have I ever had the need to market myself or the services I provide. As unbelievable as that may sound, it's true. I've never needed to.

I remember ministering at a conference once, which, at the time, was one of the largest audiences I had ever ministered before. As I walked into the arena, I stood just to the left of the stage and looked out into the faces of ten thousand beautiful individuals, each hungering for the presence of the Spirit within their lives. I can still so vividly remember thinking, in that moment, "How did I even get here?" From very humble beginnings in the prophetic ministry, it seemed so very unbelievable to most that I would even be included on the roster, at that time. However, the opportunity had come to me. I didn't ask for it. Now, all these years later, such conferences and such audiences are the norm within my life. What an amazing privilege and honor to have the ability – and most of all to be able to recognize the ability –

pg. 152

to create my life and to attract into my life path the dreams of God within me. As I prepared to take the stage and to minister, I felt the unction of the spirit within, saying, "You birthed this into manifestation." My friend, never despise your own creation process. Never, even for a moment, believe that the dreams and the inner visions you have – the internal imagery – seems outlandish or unattainable. You'll be surprised to quickly find out that not only are the dreams very attainable and very easily accessible, as you put into practice the power of your own creative knowledge, but you will then be forced to dream even larger dreams. I remember counseling a gentleman once, in a life coaching session for Identity Network, who had felt drawn to me to discuss the launch of his own company. For him, at the time, the dream to begin again seemed very, very unattainable, to put it mildly. Only six months prior, he has found himself standing upon the brink of bankruptcy. Financial advisors and even other so-called "prophets" had told him that, although he should believe in his vision of beginning a business, he should wait at least seven years before even considering starting to rebuild again. He said that after hearing my teaching entitled *Now Is Your Moment* he had felt compelled to reach out to me, and I'm so very glad that he did. Within three months of putting the power of visualization into practice, not only had he successfully launched the business but he had attracted into his life the investors needed to accomplish the task. In other words, not only were the resources drawn to him but even the right people of influence had been drawn to him.

The passage of scripture regarding the wealth of Solomon shares with us that not only did he attain great wealth through knowledge, but that even the kings of the earth had been drawn to by his mere "presence." Did you know that because of your thinking you are literally creating a magnetic force around you at all times? You might say, "Jeremy, that sounds so extreme." However, it is a known fact – not only scientifically speaking, as we have already discussed, but also in a very literal spiritual sense. I want to share with you something that, when I realized it all those years ago, not only changed my life but has since changed the lives of millions of individuals from throughout the world. "When we become determined to manifest our creative power within the earth realm, we build a more magnetic presence around us to attract what we desire." There's so much talk within Christendom about the proclamation of the gospel, and rightfully so. However, my friend, have you stopped to consider what the gospel truly is? What it truly represents to humanity? Yes, there should always be emphasis upon the majestic power of Christ, within, just as Paul spoke of, when he

pg. 156

expressed, "To whom God would make known what is the riches of the glory of this mystery among the Gentiles; which is Christ in you, the hope of glory." (Colossians 1:27) The term "gentiles" within the passage refers to the entirety of the known world of that day. The gospel is the great inner work, which makes known to the world the riches of the glory of God within the earth realm. This is why Jesus taught humanity to pray in Matthew 6:10, "Thy kingdom come, Thy will be done in earth, as it is in heaven."

The preaching of the gospel has always, in the larger sense, been about the creation of the kingdom of heaven within the earth and the

pg. 157

establishment and operation of the universal laws of Christ in this physical realm. You might ask, "So, what does this have to do with having a magnetic presence?" Those who actively study Biblical prophecy or, what some erroneously term, "end time" events, always place such special emphasis upon the twenty-fourth chapter of the gospel according to Matthew. In fact, in all honesty, this passage is perhaps the single most misquoted and most misused scripture concerning prophecy and what is to come. Allow me to explain, my friend. According to Matthew 24:3, "And as he sat upon the mount Olives, the disciples came unto him privately, saying, Tell us, when shall these things be? And what shall be the sign of thy coming and of the end of the world?" Being that this account transpires atop the Mount of Olives, this passage is commonly referred to by theologians and those who study eschatology as "The Olivet Discourse." However, the terms used within the original language reveal something much, much more powerful than any fear-based attempt to erroneously frighten the masses. Not once did the disciples truly ever ask Jesus about a second coming in the clouds or about the destructive end of the physical world. The term incorrectly translated as "coming" is the Greek term "Parousia." The term incorrectly transcribed as "world" is the Greek term "aeon," literally meaning "current age." Interestingly enough, "Parousia" is

pg. 159

defined, literally as "Presence." In other words, the disciples that day asked, "What shall be the sign of your presence?" Jesus responds, quite simply, in Matthew 24:14, but saying, "And this gospel of the kingdom shall be preached in all the world for a witness unto all nations; and then shall the end come."

I often find it quite humorous when I hear believers speak so fearfully of the "new age." Because of the truth of Christ, we are literally, even now, within a very "new age," and, contrary to what psychics, mediums, and Spiritualists claim, the true "new age" has nothing to do with their occultic practices and literally everything to do with possessing a magnetic "presence" which attracts into the earth realm the things of heaven and creates the kingdom here and now. My friend, you are magnetically attracting a life around you, even now, by your very presence. Just as kings were drawn to the presence of Solomon, so, too, is the entire world around you being drawn to the energy you are now radiating, based entirely upon your thoughts and intentions. Not only is it the riches of the glory of God for you to enact your creative power within the earth realm, but it is the very heart of the Godhead. Contrary to the popular belief of religion, you are continually establishing a kingdom with each and every thought you vibrate.

Either the kingdom you are establishing within the earth is one of the riches and glory of heaven in the earth – one of unlimited abundance and resource – or it is one based within the "old age" of thinking with old paradigms of an old consciousness. My friend, step into the "new age" of Christ Jesus and begin to attract the full measure of the riches and glory of the kingdom of God into your life. Become a conscious creator, always mindful of the presence you are radiating. Your very presence is a sort of homing beacon for the universe, by which all of heaven and all of earth are pulled to the decree of your thoughts. You are making a decree and establishing a kingdom with each passing thought, and the universe is

pg. 162

always seeking to bow down to the decree and command you make. Whether you realize it or not, the universe is actually quite obedient. Not once has it ever failed to deliver the intentions of our hearts. My friend, the universe has always bowed down to each and every decree you have ever established within your thoughts. Your life is now the product of the decrees of ages passed. Why not step into the "new age" of Christ and establish the kingdom of abundance you were always intended to create?

POWER OF EXISTENCE

With a cry, a baby is brought forth from the womb of the mother, pulled forcefully into the open air of earth. Within mere moments, all five of the natural senses begin to take full effect. There are sights and sounds which seem so very unfamiliar and frightening. The blinding, bright light overhead within the cold hospital room seems strangely familiar though – oddly reminiscent of the state of existence experienced and lived only nine months prior. Nine months after conception, another very old soul is given the opportunity to experience the earth realm. And with the joyful tears of the mother and the congratulatory remarks of the delivering physician, a powerful creator is welcomed into the physical plane of being, in order to experience the physical world for, when compared to eternity, a very brief time. You are a very old and wise soul. Before time ever even began, you *were*. Millennia before your biological father and mother were ever even conceived you existed in absolute perfection – at one with God. At the moment of conception, that powerful and Divine moment at which life embarks upon its journey toward incarnation into human flesh, the divine mind, which had existed in such harmony with the Great Creator,

pg. 166

entered into a world of physicality and immediately began to become forgetful.

For the eternal soul, although it was merely another journey through the realm of Spirit, this journey would be much, much different. In this journey, there would often be pain and heartache. There would, at times, be the great sense of loss. There would be the pain of experiencing the death of loved ones. There would be the physical pain of growing old – there would be the process of decay. Still, though, there would be happy moments as well. There would be the first kiss. There would be the joy of raising a family. There would be the limitless joy of learning. There would be music.

And though there would be equally as many pains as there would be joys, it would all exist for a very divine purpose. The soul would experience life. You see, my friend, even now you are continuing to experience a never ending journey of creation. You – the real you – existed long before you ever came into this three-dimensional plane and you will continue to exist long, long after you take your final breath within the physical body you now inhabit. I try to paint this imagery for you as best I know how to simply say that there is so much more to you than what you realize.

Many say that the moment we are born, we begin to die. In the physical sense this statement is true, only in that it refers to the state of the physical body. The physical body, however, has never at any time been the true and authentic *you*. You are an eternal spirit and never once have you ever experienced death in any way. The truth of the matter is that it is impossible for the true you to ever die. In Ephesians 2:5-7, Paul writes, "Even when we were dead in sins, hath quickened us together with Christ, (by grace ye are saved;) and hath raised us up together, and made us sit together in heavenly places in Christ Jesus: That in the ages to come he might shew the exceeding riches of his grace in his kindness toward us through Christ Jesus." You see, my friend, even the scriptures bear out that you have always

pg. 169

been a very old soul – existing long before and long after the end of the physical body. As the Lord spoke through Jeremiah, in Jeremiah 1:5, "Before I formed thee in the belly I knew thee; and before thou camest forth out of the womb I sanctified thee, and I ordained thee a prophet unto the nations." At no point have you ever been separated from the Godhead, because by your very nature you are an eternal, powerful spirit. Remarkable, however, is the use of the term "knew," within the passage of Jeremiah. Not only does the very text suggest that we were known by God and were experiencing the creative power of God long, long before ever incarnating into human flesh, it suggests, even more so, that we were co-creators with him

pg. 170

from the very beginning. In fact, in Genesis 1:26, we find our eternal existence stated in this way: "And God said, Let us make man in our image, after our likeness: and let them have dominion over the fish of the sea, and over the fowl of the air, and over the cattle, and over all the earth, and over every creeping thing that creepeth upon the earth." The passage begs the question, who are the "us" God was referring to when he said, "Let *us* make man in our image?" You see, in order to truly understand the creative power which you possess within the earth realm we must, first, come to terms with the very real fact that creative power has always been vital to our very eternal existence.

In the passage of Jeremiah, when the Lord says that he "knew" you, the term in the original Hebrew is "YADA," quite literally meaning "to know in an intimate way." Knowing this, you will find it remarkable that in the account, detailed in Luke 1:34, when the angel of the Lord appears to Mary to announce that she would bring forth a child, her response is that she had never "known" a man. "Then said Mary unto the angel, How shall this be, seeing I *know* not a man?" She was referring, of course, to sexual intimacy. The translation of the New American Standard Bible states it in this way: "Mary said to the angel, "How can this be, since I am a virgin?" As we know, true intimacy is, in itself, a very creative power. It

pg. 172

recreates. It produces offspring. It causes life to come forth. Shall I say it another way? Your very existence is a command of God to create within the earth realm. To prove this point even further, let us examine the very words of Jesus, himself. The text Matthew 7:21-23 further bears out the command of God to create. In the words of Jesus, "Not every one that saith unto me, Lord, Lord, shall enter into the kingdom of heaven; but he that doeth the will of my Father which is in heaven. Many will say to me in that day, Lord, Lord, have we not prophesied in thy name? and in thy name have cast out devils? And in thy name done many wonderful works? And then I will profess unto them, I never *knew* you: depart from me, ye that work iniquity." To

pg. 173

put it much more plainly, "You and I never *created* anything together."

Do you realize, now, just how vital your creative process is, not only to the physical world but, even more so, to the unseen, spiritual world and the afterlife? When a child comes forth from the womb of the mother, in the natural world, biologically speaking, the child possesses the DNA of the earthly father. There is no escaping this truth. The same, though, could be said within the spiritual sense. Your very existence within this world is proof-positive that you possess the DNA of creation within your very being, even now. As I shared in my book, *Abandoned to Divine Destiny*,

pg. 174

"Before there was anything – before there was even nothing – in a time predating time, and a space beyond time – when only two things existed, God and you – there were not two things at all. There was actually only One." My friend, your very existence within the physical plane of the earth realm represents the Oneness of a co-creative energy. There is a symbiotic union being enacted at all times – a divine partnership of creation, if you will. This Oneness far transcends the limiting man-made interpretations of human theology. It is, much rather, a very definitive truth of the law of creation. You are one with God. Your power to create is in harmony with the creative power of God. The very identity of God is encapsulated into your very being, as a co-creator with the Godhead. Remember that literally everything we find in scripture relating to the essence if God is related, in a very definitive way, to the very essence which you possess, for "as he is, so are we in this world." (1 John 4:17)

I learned very early on when beginning to uncover the deeper mysteries and cycles and patterns of universal law found contained within scripture that it has always been the intention of the mind of the Spirit to reveal to us the creative essence of God within. Everything concerning the kingdom of God is contained *within*. It is the internal nature of God, within, which shapes and creates the physical world, without –

externally. At the moment of birth, as you entered into this sphere of reality – the physical, three-dimensional, illusionary world of time and space – the five senses began to collect all manner of data. You would soon realize that you enjoy the taste of ice cream and that you love the feeling of holding onto your significant other. You would come to realize how good it feels to give and receive love. You would realize how very good it feels to give away and to become a blessing to others. In other words, you began to make decrees and laws within the earth, by your very existence here, which would begin to define your relation to the physical world around you. The creative mind, acting within the realm of the five, natural senses, began to collect data and information daily for you, by which you would begin to live. Habits would form. Ideas and beliefs would begin to take shape, as a result of certain experiences. In the acclaimed and historic book, *Man's Search for Meaning*, by Viktor E. Frankl, the author says, "Those who have a 'why' to live, can bear with almost any 'how.'" As profound as such a statement might seem, the statement seems of far more significance, when knowing that Frankl was, himself, a captive of Auschwitz, during the Holocaust. Seeing so many die around him, including his own family, he began to ask the greater, deeper questions of life.

Why is it that some can remain trapped within circumstance while others are able to, as Abraham Maslow says, "self-actualize?" Frankl would go on to say, "Ultimately, man should not ask what the meaning of his life is, but rather must recognize that it is he who is asked. In a word, each man is questioned by life; and he can only answer to life by answering for his own life; to life he can only respond by being responsible." What a beautiful truth from a great mind who had endured such tremendous hardship and unspeakable agony. Frankl suggests that is up to the individual to assume personal responsibility for self-actualization – self-awakening – and the untethering of the consciousness from old, limiting mindsets. The

pg. 179

phrase "This is the way I am" is so very limiting. It is a complete misnomer. Who you are is eternal and creative in nature and, as such, who you are can always be changed. Your conditioning is fluid and not concrete. To change the conditioning of the mind, it is necessary to understand that the mind can be entirely reconditioned through continued self-actualization – personal accountability not only to the thought possessed but, also, to the reasons behind the thought. You see, never once have you been apart or outside of your own creative process. Your very existence is now an extension of the Godhead within the earth realm and, contrary to the faulty and erroneous and divisive teachings of religion, never at any point

pg. 180

have you truly been separated from God. We are separated only within our minds.

It is important to bear in mind that within the Garden, there was no tree of "good" and "evil." Rather, there was a tree of the "knowledge" of "good" and "evil." Yet, even after partaking of the fruit and succumbing consciously to the illusionary idea of separation – becoming forgetful of who they were – the Lord still continued to come to walk with man within the cool of the day. Separation has never existed. It is, quite simply, a religious concept of division. Christ Jesus came to remind all of humanity of the eternal Oneness which had always existed. It is for this reason that so often within the New Testament writings ministry is referred to as "reconciliation." Reconcile within your mind – reconnect – and remember the truth of your eternal existence and the power of your eternal, creative force. With the firing of each and every synapse of your brain, all of creation is continuing to bow down to the decrees and the laws which you are establishing, and like attracts like. My friend, there is a very real reason why you are the way you are and why you now find yourself within the state of being which you do. Own it. Accept responsibility. As painful and as difficult as it is to fathom, you have always been a part of your own, creative processes. In a moment – in the "twinkling" of an eye – all of it can be changed. The creative

mind   can   become   awakened.

CREATIVE SHIFTING

The renewal of the mind is a process which can begin in a moment but continues indefinitely. When Pauline epistles were written to the early churches still under formation, I am absolutely convinced that the "renewing of the mind" he spoke of was intended to depict a continuous, ongoing, and never ending process. In Pauline epistles, it is interesting to note much of the terminology used to illustrate a "process." So often, in the text of his letters to the early churches, Paul looked to a future time at which believers would come to a point of maturity. His epistles depicted the process of continual growth and change rapidly occurring within the minds of the early believers. Allow me to give a few examples of what I mean by this. In his first epistle to the church at Corinth, Paul admonishes, "Brethren, be not children in understanding; howbeit in malice be ye children, but in understanding be men." (1 Corinthians 14:20) The New Living Translation of the Bible states it in this manner: "Dear brothers and sisters, don't be childish in your understanding of these things. Be innocent as babies when it comes to evil, but be mature in understanding matters of this kind." In his epistle to the church at Ephesus, Paul says, ""That we henceforth be no more children, tossed to and fro, and carried about with every wind of doctrine, by the sleight of men, and cunning craftiness, whereby they lie in wait to deceive. But speaking the truth in love, may grow up into him in all things, which is the head, even Christ." (Ephesians 4:14-15)

The writer of Hebrews admonishes believers in this way: "Therefore leaving the principles of the doctrine of Christ, let us go on unto perfection." (Hebrews 6:1) In other words, renewal is a continuous and ongoing process of growing up – moving beyond vain religious dogma and the traditions of men to become mature in the *knowledge* of Christ. As unfortunate as it might seem, how very often have we encountered many sincere believers spend years debating useless dogma, literally being tossed about by doctrine, only to never truly accomplish very much within their lives for the kingdom of God? My friend, with no offence, maturity has absolutely nothing to do with physical age. The ability to defend the doctrines of your church means very little within the kingdom of God. The Apostles were continuously encouraging growth within the Spirit – moving beyond elementary, childish teachings and coming to a full understanding of the truth of Christ within. In other words, we are admonished continuously to "grow up" in our knowledge and understanding of the things of God, in order to better enact the creation of the kingdom within this dimension of time and space within the physical world.

Whether you've realized it yet or not, life in the Spirit is a continuous series of shifts. Therein lies the power of creation at work. Although we are not allowed to undo the past, we are given every opportunity to recreate a better, more fulfilling present and future by beginning to manifest much more responsibly with our thoughts. There is a very divine principle concerning the law of agreement which helps us to better understand the continuous cycle of growth we are experiencing, day by day. In Matthew 18:19, Jesus says, "Again I say unto you, That if two of you shall agree on earth as touching any thing that they shall ask, it shall be done for them of my Father which is in Heaven." Scripture makes it very plain that there is divine power in agreement – both corporate agreement and personal agreement. You might be asking what I mean by "personal" agreement. I'm referring to the agreements we make with ourselves – consciously and subconsciously. Did you know that with each and every thought you are actually making an agreement with yourself? Your entire life has been a series of agreements in some way or another. You've agreed either to accept and adapt or you've agreed to advance and accelerate. Either way, you've made more agreements than you realize.

Let's examine this law of agreement more closely to better understand. What we accept, we adapt to. This is why some wait for years before ever beginning to enact change;

that is, if they ever even begin to enact change at all. For those who do finally awaken within – even after years of having accepted and adapted – they finally begin to advance and move forward into greater revelatory truth and into a greater dimension of creative power. They begin to accelerate. Shall I say, they finally begin to "grow up" into the greater knowledge of the inner Christ. When speaking of the law of attraction at work, I always make it a point to urge caution and a word of warning. I do so not to incite a sense of fear within you but, rather, to inspire a greater sense of personal responsibility.

Neurons of the brain connect very quickly, as we've discussed. Almost instantly, they begin to establish laws and decrees within the body. The mouth will only speak what the mind believes and can fathom. The body will respond to the conditioning of the thoughts within the mind. For this reason, it is vitally important that we remain conscious – ever-conscious – of our thoughts. With each thought, in each and every experience, the new neural pathways are being formed within the brain and the brain, itself, is being molded to further enact the same feelings. This is why not only are old patterns and old paradigms of thinking difficult to change but also why many habits are difficult to break. However, be encouraged, my friend. Difficult has never meant impossible.

Just as the habit or the belief began with a singular thought, so, too, does the renewal process also begin with just a single, awakened thought of change. Growth and maturity into greater depths of creative power begin in an instant. Did you know that your entire body will heed the words and commands that you give it? Even when you are consciously unaware of the decrees and commands you are giving? The physical, human form, just like the universe, is always very obedient. I share greater details of this fact in my course on divine healing and will share much more soon; however, when addressing the importance of shifting in order to attract, suffice it to say that in order to shift something new in, something old must be shifted out. Your daily life is a series of conscious shifts, continually ongoing, depending entirely upon what your focus is placed upon. There is also, at all times, a type of spiritual inertia – a momentum – which exists behind each and every subtle shift.

In other words, your thoughts begin to gain speed. Let's look at this divine universal principle of agreement with the Self in a much more practical way, to make it relatable. The man who awakens in the morning to an argument with his spouse or to a call of unexpectedly, negative news will absolutely in no way share the same creative energy of a man who awakens each morning to a moment of mindfulness and meditation and contemplation. The energies are much different, therefore setting different tones for the day ahead.

Think of it this way. How often have you awakened to the day in a moment of stress or negativity, only to find that throughout the day you found only more of the same negativity? So many speak of the presence of God, yet have absolutely no clue about how to be truly present themselves. I was speaking to a young woman once who had attended a conference in which I taught the power of visualization, and she informed me of an accident she had once had while driving. To many, it would have seemed to be a day like any other day. For her, there was to be the same, daily routine and the same daily responsibilities. However, upon closer examination, something was actually much different that day, even starting out. "My husband and I had a heated argument that morning," she explained. "Then I was late taking the kids to school." "Traffic seemed worse than usual that day." She went on to say, "I was late for work and my mind was elsewhere. I just wasn't paying attention." You see, the energy of those beginning moments had quite literally set the tone for her entire day ahead. She admitted to me that she had allowed the heated argument which had begun her day to literally follow her throughout the rest of the day. The energy continued to build – the thoughts began to pick up speed. Momentum was beginning to build – in the wrong direction. The result could have been deadly. That's why it's so very, very important to begin your day with the right, focused intention.

The psalmist shared in Psalm 63:1, "O God, early will I seek thee." My friend, you can't sleep the entire day away and expect to be successful. Cycles of time within this dimension exists for a very real reason, and part of learning to be personally responsible for your creative power means learning to better manage your time throughout the day. Each morning, I awaken early, most of the time before sunrise, and I either go for a walk or sit within my meditation garden, and I set the intention of my day ahead. There is absolutely no business conducted during those hours. In fact, I won't allow it. If I receive a call during that time, I send it directly to voicemail. I do that not to be rude in any way but, rather, because I know full well the power of beginning a day with the proper intention of mindfulness. My friend, nothing is more important to you than you inner sense of peace. Without it, your entire creation will be out of alignment. In order to create a masterpiece throughout the day, begin with a blank canvas each morning, early – long before the stresses and burdens of the day can begin. I promise you, this simple principle will not only change your day, it will make you exponentially more productive. In turn, you will manifest greater wealth and abundance because you will enter into the day with the proper mindfulness. Always make time for people, but never so at the expense of your own mindfulness.

"What you allow is what will remain." This simple yet transcendent truth is in many ways essential to the process of beginning to shift into the greater revelatory knowledge of God and harnessing the creative power of the universe for the purposes of your own creation. Beloved, one of the most difficult and, quite possibly, painful truths to accept is recognizing that you could have changed your life years ago. The recognition of this may hurt. It may cause you to feel as though so much time has been wasted. However, as painful as it is to recognize that you could have changed your life years ago, the greatest and most beautiful feeling is realizing that you can begin to change right now. Actually, from the perspective of the Sprit, there are no wastes of time. Your experiences are now your testimony and your pains the fuel by which you are now being propelled into a brighter destiny ahead. It's all served a purpose – even those years that you may now feel were such wasted years.

Through the prophet Joel, the Lord declares, "And I will restore to you the years that the locust hath eaten, the cankerworm, and the caterpillar, and the palmerworm, my great army which I sent among you." (Joel 2:25) Today, you can begin to accelerate into your creative power. You can begin to build speed again and recover all the years that to you now seem so very wasted. You can recover from years of careless creations by beginning to put into practice the divine laws of God interwoven throughout the fabric of the universe, beginning today. Isn't it interesting to note, however, that in Joel 2:25, the Lord refers to the destructive forces as his own, "great army" which he, himself, was responsible for sending? Needless to say, my friend, the entire universe has always been attempting to capture your attention. The force of destruction, the loss, and the lack were all, in some divine way, tools in the hand of God. Because of your innate, creative power, the universe did not wish to allow you to remain where you were. The Spirit loves you far too much to allow you to remain in your old, destructive mindsets of the past. The destruction was allowed, simply to awaken – simply that you might begin to shift.

MAKING ROOM

"But we all, with open face beholding as in a glass the glory of the Lord, are changed into the same image from glory to glory, even as by the Spirit of the Lord." – 2 Corinthians 3:18

Do you desire the *good*, or do you desire the *great*? In case you haven't realized it yet, what you are willing to allow, you are consciously accepting. You are consciously agreeing to. I sense, though, that you are now entering a time of great inner restlessness – a great inner stirring – as the inner man becomes awakened and emboldened with the power of creation's call. Even now, in this moment of time, a new mantle for powerful creation is resting upon you, the likes of which you have never experienced before. It is the call of the creator, within. It is the full awakening of the inner Christ. For far too long, you have been made to believe that you are simply the product of happenstance or chance and that the unseen hands of fate or chance or destiny have controlled you without accepting any input from you. The truth of the matter is that there are very real unseen forces, as we have discussed, but that the unseen forces of energy – the vibrational, creative power of God within – has always been at your command, according to your own will and thought. Now, though, your knowledge is changing. A great light has come. The old things have passed away and all things are beginning to be made new, even now, in this moment. The spark of creative power, which at the beginning of time illuminated the cosmos, is now the awakening within you. The mighty God in Christ has now become the Christ in you. With that awakening has come the full measure of the truth of identity. No longer are you going to be able to be content with hapless, careless, creation practices. No, you are now going to begin to become more aware of each and every thought and each and every action, viewing your thoughts as choices and decrees which the universe – the material world around you – has absolutely no choice but to succumb to. This is the new beginning – now – in this moment. The term *Kairos*, in Greek, is often used within scripture to denote moments of time. However, it is not used to denote the passing of time, as we have become familiar with the passing of time. It denotes, rather, an instantaneous moment of creative time. An instantaneous moment at which change begins to occur – a literal paradigm shift. Change occurs, within, at the moment of conscious recognition of truth. You see, it is always at the moment of recognition that change begins to truly occur and the seeds of truth begin to blossom forth from within. The issue has never been a matter of truth, my friend. The issue has always been man's ability or inability to recognize truth. "You shall know the

truth, and the truth shall make you free."
It's not the truth which frees; it's the
truth you know and recognize which
makes you free. At the moment of full
recognition – spiritual awakening – a
release begins to occur. Chains become
broken. It's as if the prison doors within
the mind are opened by angelic forces.
However, unless you choose to walk
through the opened doorway into your
newfound freedom, you will still be a
captive prisoner by your own choice.
Unchained locks and opened prison
doors mean absolutely nothing if the
captive – the prisoner within – does not

choose to walk through the portal into the newness of life being given.

Above all, it is my passionate and burning hope that you can begin to realize just how incredibly free you are. You always have been. The prison within the mind has been the illusion by which you have lived so very much of your life. Much of your creation has been enacted through the filtered lens of dogma and disconnectedness. The same could be said of each of us, at times. Yet, when awakening comes – when the Spirit of truth comes – and when revelatory knowledge comes, a choice is made within the mind. Will I accept the truth or will I continue to live within the old pattern? The power which you possess is quite an inconvenient truth, is it not? For you, the recognition of such unlimited and untethered power might seem quite daunting – like much more of a curse than a blessing. For so many within humanity, when they first begin to come to the fullness of an awakened mind, there is that momentary sense of feeling overwhelmed. The mind that has spent a lifetime choosing to blame rather than taking responsibility is burdened by the inconvenient truth of the knowledge of personal, creative power. It's always so much more easy – much more convenient – to blame others, is it not? To blame the universe, to blame God, and to blame others around us for our own inability – I should say unwillingness – to self-actualize. Awakening is quite painful, for a moment. It is as the pain of childbirth – intense and filled with bouts of agony – as the old mind is reshaped, reconditioned, and reformed. We lose the sense of familiarity and our old systems of beliefs. There is the momentary bleeding that occurs – the old paradigm is laid waste to, as a new birth begins. Then, in the newness of life – within the new paradigm we find ourselves in, there is nothing but joy. The joy of the new birth, then, far outweighs the pain and agony of the birthing process.

Today, my friend, I wish to encourage you to never settle for the status quo of religious isolationism, which has for far too long sought to keep you imprisoned to your own demises of your own past creations. No, you are not merely a depraved sinner saved by grace. It is, rather, because of that grace that you are now being given the ability to move beyond, into far greater glories of creative power than you could have once even dreamed. With awakening comes a new, greater vision and an even greater dream. I realized early on, when beginning my professional work within the prophetic, the vast power we possess to not only call things into being but, more importantly, to call things which have been for so long out of alignment, back into divine alignment. If you think about it, in truth, the process of the new birth is quite literally a coming back into alignment – a remembering of the true nature once forgotten within the garden, when mankind began to forget its true and divine nature as powerful spirit beings that were given dominion over all the earth. The awakening of the mind within – the creative vibration of God – is the moment at which you return to divine alignment. It's the moment you remember the unlimited power and the unlimited resources you were destined to possess – and never truly lost to begin with. "Wherefore I put thee in remembrance that thou stir up the gift of God which is in thee by the putting on of my hand." (2 Timothy 1:6) The New International Version translation says, more literally, to "fan into flames" the inner gift of God that we possess.

There's so much to be said of the inner gift of creative power which we possess. The *charism* – or gift – is an endowment of power innate within all believers, lying dormant until it first be recognized and then activated. Within Christendom – particularly within charismatic circles – there is often much talk of miraculous, superhuman power because of the anointing. However, the anointing upon you means very little until you first begin to recognize the anointing within you for greater works. Jesus spoke of the creative power and the inner anointing in this way, in John 14:12: "Verily, verily I say unto you, He that believeth on me, the works that I do shall he do also; and greater works than these shall he do; because I go unto my Father." For generations, we've been told that "greater works" means greater in type or greater in quality. However, this cannot possibly be the case. When was the last time you went to a funeral and commanded a corpse to live, bringing it back to life? Has it been a while? When was the last time you walked on water? You see, we must begin to reexamine our idea of the miraculous. When Jesus was speaking to his followers of "greater works," he was not referring to "greater" in the quality of work or "greater" in the type of miraculous power. He was referring to greater in duration. If I were to paraphrase, Jesus was, in fact, saying, "I'm only here for a short time, then it's your turn." Now, generations later, it's your turn to begin using your own creative power to manifest the kingdom of God within the earth realm by realizing that you are creating the world around you with your thoughts. **Jesus is no longer here physically. Now it's your turn.**

When we begin to think of the creative power which we possess – the creative power of the Kingdom of God within – it is vitally important that we recognize we are continually being moved into greater dimensions of knowledge. With greater understanding comes a new paradigm of thinking and greater revelatory knowledge, which causes us to become emboldened and to begin to dream even greater dreams. The process of creation within our lives is a process of constantly-expanding, ever-changing scenery. My friend, if the scenery around you is never changing, it in no way means that you're being faithful – it simply means you aren't going anywhere. It means there's no movement. How long have we viewed a lack of changing scenery as faithfulness? "I'm here because God put me here." "I'm here because this is where God planted me." Even the most beautiful plants have inner movement, causing them to blossom forth into new, creative life. Do you recall, in Mark chapter 11, when Jesus cursed the fig tree? This passage of scripture is one of the most compelling cases for the power of creation and the law of attraction working within one's life. According to the New International Version translation of the text, "The next day as they were leaving Bethany, Jesus was hungry. Seeing in the distance a fig tree in leaf, he went to find out if it had any fruit. When he reached it, he found nothing but leaves, because it was not the season for figs. Then he said to the tree, "May no one ever eat fruit from you again." And his disciples heard him say it. In the morning, as they went along, they saw the fig tree withered from the roots. Peter remembered and said to Jesus, Rabbi, look! The fig tree you cursed has withered!" "Have faith in God," Jesus answered. "Truly I tell you, if anyone says to this mountain, 'Go, throw yourself into the sea,' and does not doubt in their heart but believes what they say will happen, it will be done for them." (Mark 11: 12-14, 19-23) This passage clearly indicates the literal creative force behind our focused intention – it reveals the importance of harnessing the power of one's own will. Throughout years of prophetic ministry, I've heard various interpretations of this text from ministers throughout the world. Some have even gone as far as to say that the account was nothing more Jesus throwing a temper tantrum, because the fig tree hadn't given him what he wanted. No, my friend, nothing could be any more untrue. If one pays particularly close attention to the text, one would find that it wasn't even the season for figs in the first place! There are two very important prophetic principles being enacted within this account. First, the fig tree represents deception within certain seasons of time. Notice that although it was not the season for figs, the tree *appeared* to be blossoming. There were leaves upon it which, to the natural eye, indicated that there should also be fruit. However, it was fruitless. There are many people – many sincere believers – who have been deceived for far too long. As a result, on the surface, they appear to be faithful. They appear to be planted firmly. They appear to be productive. However, they are bearing no fruit. They are *creating nothing.* Secondly, even more importantly, there is the powerful prophetic principle of desire. By cursing the fig tree, Jesus was illustrating to his disciples that we have the divine right and the divine power to get what we want, regardless of the season we find ourselves in. *You have the power to get exactly what you want, exactly when you want it.*

Religion creates such a dichotomy within the mind – a very real bipolar nature, if you will. Because of this, it inundates the mind of humanity with a sort of paranoid schizophrenia – a very real, continuous fear. "Is this the will of God?" "Is this the will of God or is it my will?" "Am I in the perfect will of God or the permissive will of God?" It's such nonsense, really. Is it any wonder the religious mind is so crippling? I so often see and hear many wonderful individuals living lives of worry, expressing such words of fear and doubt and unbelief, all because they have failed to recognize that they are an extension of God within the earth realm – the Lord of all the earth. *Because of Christ, the will of God is not separate from the will of the believer – there are no longer two wills, but one, singular will being enacted.* To fully begin to enact conscious creative power within this dimension of the physical world, begin to recognize that your very essence is, in fact, the very will of God. In fact, because of Christ, you could not be separated from his will no matter how hard you tried. That is, unless you are refusing to manifest the life you truly desire, in which case you are left to your own demises, the byproduct of legalism and the systems of this world. My friend, you are *in* this world but never once have you ever truly been *of* this world. This physical plane is merely a temporary residence in which you are given the opportunity to explore, to create, and to enjoy the fullness of the creative mind of God which we possess.

My friend, in order to begin to attract the new life you so desperately desire, you must begin to make room for your manifestation. As the scriptures make perfectly clear and bear out, something "new" will never fit into something "old." In Matthew 9:17, Jesus shares the principle of the "new" in this way: "Neither do men put new wine into old bottles: else the bottles break, and the wine runneth out, and the bottles perish: but they put new wine into new bottles, and both are preserved." In order to manifest and to maintain the new life you are truly desire, you must begin to accommodate your creation. In other words, you must make room for the life you truly desire. Manifestation requires rearrangement. In my teaching *The Beginning Stages of Attracting* I describe how conscious manifestation is actually quite a strategic process for the awakened. It requires sensitivity and careful maneuvering. Maneuvering which, in itself, requires even greater sensitivity. Allow me to explain. Far, far too often, we fail to dream new dreams simply because we are holding onto the dreams of the past – refusing to let go. We speak so often of the "glory days" and the accomplishments of times long passed. We think back, so often, with familiarity, at all that we accomplished in certain seasons of time within our lives and ask, "Why can't it be like that again?" Well, the truth of the matter, my friend, is that it isn't supposed to be like *that* again. This is a new day. This is a new season. A new vision for a new age within one's life requires the ability to move beyond the old dreams and visions of the past ages. Without this ability to move beyond – the innate ability to transcend into even greater glories – we become imprisoned and bound by chains to the past. We, in turn, begin to feel a sense of hopelessness, rather than faith, because we tell ourselves it will never happen again, like it did, "back then." In this life, you will either be a prisoner of the past or a visionary of the future, at peace within the present. There is no other way to be. The success you so enjoyed long ago in a former season of your life was specifically for that season. The relationships which surrounded you then were specifically for that season –

pg. 233

that moment of time. Stop attempting to cling to the old when the "new" awaits you. Stop living within past victories and begin to conquer the new day dawning by dreaming an even greater vision. Do you want the "good" or do you want the "great?" Both cannot coexist simultaneously. In order to attain the new, you must recognize that the old – as wonderful as it might have seemed at the time – has long-since passed away. Far too often we fail to give new birth to new and greater visions because we, instead, cling to the corpses of the old, dead dreams of the past.

Few verses of scripture illustrate the damning consequences of holding onto past success quite like the passage of scripture found within the book of Numbers, chapter 21. "And Moses made a serpent of brass, and put it upon a pole, and it came to pass, that if a serpent had bitten any man, when he beheld the serpent of brass, he lived." (Numbers 21:9) Commanded by God to create a point of contact – a focal point – for the people, Moses fashioned the brazen serpent as a symbol of healing for all who had been bitten by venomous serpents. However, within the book of Kings, we find that many had come to worship the image as an idol. The brazen serpent, or *Nehushtan*, had become a false god and pagan idol. In other words, even the successes and blessings in life, when not moved beyond in new seasons, become little more than curses which hold us back. How often have you made the successes of your past an idol to be worshipped? My friend, just because it worked for you then doesn't mean it will work for you now. It isn't supposed to. Its usefulness to you ended as the season changed. Now, in this season of your life, it is time for new revelatory knowledge and a new awakening to match the new frontier of creation you now find yourself living within. In this season of attracting the life you truly desire, you will begin to attract new points of contact, new connections, new investors for business, and new relationships which will serve you for this season. Then, in an instant, at some future point of time, the season will then change again. This is why spiritual sensitivity is so vitally important within the process of attracting – specifically within the beginning stages of attracting. We must learn to discern the ever-changing energies at work around us. In Matthew 16:3, Jesus rebukes the

Pharisees – the religious leaders of the time – saying, "O ye hypocrites, ye can discern the face of the sky; but can ye not discern the signs of the times?" It takes a continuous awakening in order to correctly discern the ever-changing energies of creation being enacted around us. In order to truly be successful and consciously attract the life you truly desire, it is vitally important that you be able to know when it is time to move on. Moving on doesn't equate to failure; it equates to maturity and growth. You are living in dreams you outgrew years ago, my friend. You are living with the desires of yesteryear. It's time to dream a new dream; but, in order to do that, you must allow yourself to let go of the victories of the past. *Stop idolizing the past and begin to create a much more powerful present.*

Scripture continuously speaks of the new age – ages to come – and future seasons of time. "That in the *ages* to come he might shew the exceeding riches of his grace in his kindness toward us through Christ Jesus." (Ephesians 2:7) Seasons are constantly changing, and, even now there are constant moments of ever-changing cycles of advancement and acceleration even within the current season you now find yourself living within. Sensitivity to the inner voice of the Spirit is essential to not only being able to discern the times and the seasons, which Jesus spoke so clearly of, but also to recognize when a "new" age has become "old." Through each ever-changing cycle, however, there is always the law of attraction at work – either pulling into the world around you a continuance of more of the same from the past or creating a brighter future of revelation and creative power and abundance through the creative mind. Either way, there truly is no escaping the principle of the law of attraction at work. You are one with God. You always have been. You always will be. It is through the enacting of your own will that you are creating,

pg. 240

because the creative power of the Godhead is, by its very nature, your own nature. Creation will never be escaped, and it is continuously ongoing in each and every moment of consciousness. You see, today, rather than heralding the former glories of the past, you are destined to step into even greater dreams – greater works – and a new glory for a new age and season of your life. The beginning stage of attracting what you truly desire is to recognize the vast importance of making room for the new manifestation. To shift the new in, you must first shift out the old. Today, my friend, there are mindsets and ideas and, yes, even people who are no longer serving you. The very things that once seemed to be such a very real blessing

pg. 241

within your life are now the very things which have become a stumbling block and a hindrance to you. My friend, it's time to begin waving farewell to the ideas and ideologies of the past. Old things have truly passed away and all things are being made new in each and every moment of time. It's *time* for you to begin recognizing it.

CLEANSING THE TEMPLE

"Know ye not that your body is the temple of the Holy Ghost which is in you, which ye have of God, and ye are not your own?" – 1 Corinthians 6:19

As we've already established, there is a very real and very tangible correlation between the state of the mind and the state of the body at all times. There is no escaping this principle. As we've learned, "As a man thinketh in his heart, so is he." Thoughts become things. The thought life is constantly and continually bending the energies and frequencies of the universe in according to our own will – based upon our inner thoughts. Because of this, I would be remiss if I did not also say to you that your thought life is directly correlated to the state of your physical, biological body, as well. In truth, there can be no denying the effects of the creative, all-powerful mind upon the physical body. As a student of the prophetic for most of my life, I've witnessed, firsthand, the effects of divine healing. It is very real. In fact, power for divine healing is, in many ways, much for real to me than even you are, because the power of the Holy Spirit is the basis of all that I do within my life and within my ministry. Throughout the years, I've witnessed, firsthand, many divine occurrences of supernatural and miraculous healing – miraculous events which baffled even the minds of doctors and caused even those in the medical field to believe in the power of the supernatural. I've witnessed tumors dissolve, before my eyes. I've watched as a man, lame from birth, received strength to stand and took his very first steps. I've watched as the wheelchairs which had confined so many individuals became emptied, as many began to walk. Yes, miraculous healing is very real, and as a prophet called of God to awaken humanity to his covenant within the earth, I must say to you that the power of the Spirit of God is a power of the miraculous in each and every way. However, for a moment, please allow me to share with you several important concepts concerning the state of the mind and the state of the body and the correlation linking the two. Let's be honest with ourselves for a moment. So very often we hear powerful, soul-stirring messages of divine healing; however, very rarely does the church ever talk about health. Health within the physical body. You see, my friend, although the miraculous is a very present reality within the lives of believers, because of the power of the inner Christ, and divine physical healing is a very well-known and documented fact, what if we truly learned to live in health, instead? Therein, again, is the underlying premise of personal responsibility – something we rarely ever wish to even speak of. You see, it's wonderful to see God heal individuals of sugar diabetes and cancer; however, what if I told you that you never had to have the disease to begin with? To ask

God to heal you, miraculously of sugar diabetes, while continuing to eat processed foods and drink six sodas a day, is not only the height of all folly but is a disgraceful hypocrisy which the church continues to sweep underneath the rug. It's never talked about. Not only is this wrong, it is disgraceful.

Today, like never before, the outside world looks upon what can only be described as the laughable, blatant hypocrisy of the church. It cannot be denied, no matter how you attempt to justify it. Having worked within Christian publishing for decades as a published, bestselling author, I can tell you that for every

Christian book addressing diet and exercise and health, there are thirty more books addressing the subject of divine healing and the miraculous. Why is this? The answer is quite simple. We refuse to take personal responsibility for our creations. We refuse to take personal responsibility for our own lives. Rather than eating a proper diet and shunning those ingredients which are known to be toxic to us, we, instead, continue to consume practically anything offered to us and then pray for God to heal us when disease comes. What an absurd way to live! According to the Book of James, a "double minded" man is unstable in all his ways. "A double minded man is unstable in all his ways." (James 1:8) According to the

pg. 249

previous verse within the text, "For let not that man think that he shall receive anything from the Lord." The New International Version translation of James 1:7 says, quite plainly, "That person should not expect to receive anything from the Lord."

My friend, so very often, what we choose to put into our temple – the human body – is absolutely disgraceful. You may find yourself now thinking, "I purchased this book to learn to create my life, not for dieting tips." Well, you see, my friend, therein is the root of the issue. Your physical body is even a very real outward manifestation of what is taking place within your mind. As uncomfortable as it might be to address, obesity and health concerns involving poor nutrition and diet are outward manifestations of ingrained patterns of behavior. Now, please know that I say this with all love and with all grace, because I know it isn't always easy. In fact, the pursuit of proper nutrition can often times feel like a daily battle. In fact, my own physician has said to me that I could stand to lose five pounds. I share this personal detail with you to simply say, it's a process that we all must become more consciously aware of and take responsibility for in our own lives.

It is absolutely absurd to even think that one can talk about the power of the law of attraction and not believe that that what we put into our bodies on a daily basis matters. *We are literally attracting disease with what we choose to put into our bodies on a daily basis.* We are literally causing our bodies to rot and to decay from the inside out. Did you know that according to the most recent statistics from the American Heart Association, the average American is inflicting damage upon their body by consuming, on average, 22 teaspoons of sugar each and every day? Yes, you read that correctly. A diet high in refined sugars can make the body much more prone to developing type 2 diabetes and insulin resistance. Refined sugars also effects mood in a very real way. According to information published in the

Public Health Journal, diets that are high in fast food and refined sugars lead to a more than forty percent higher rate of depression than those who eat a more balanced and conscientious diet. This is caused, in part, because higher insulin resistance causes lower amounts of dopamine – the "feel good" hormone. Quite literally, one of the main reasons you feel "bad" is because of what you are putting into your body. Hear me, my friend, when I say that something has to change. How can you expect to truly be sensitive to the spirit when the foods you are eating are playing tricks on your mind and your emotions? You see, processed foods are literally foods that have been manipulated to have a longer shelf-life. In other words, processed foods are not real foods – they're the creation of man. In fact, if you want to look even further into this truth, you will find that so much of what society is now labeling as "natural" food is still being genetically modified. In other words, even many of the foods being labeled as "natural" to the public are actually very "unnatural." You may ask, "What does it truly matter?" Well, first of all, it matters because it is a reflection of your own mindset. Secondly, it is a reflection of one's own sense of personal responsibility. When I was led to begin removing sugar from my diet years ago, I'll be the first to admit, it was in no way an easy process. In fact, it hurt, mainly because I had been conditioned to enjoy

pg. 254

it so much. You see, all behavior is really conditioned, learned behavior. Yes, even diet and the consumption of certain foods. Because of this, just as developing a dependence upon sugar and processed, genetically-modified foods is a learned behavior, the dependence can be just as easily unlearned through proper nutrition and exercise.

I have a friend who once told me how for so long he had begun to feel very sluggish and lethargic. According to him, he continually felt as if he "had no energy." Regardless of how must rest he got, he never could quite seem to feel rested enough. He said to me, "Jeremy, I found myself sleeping more hours and having

pg. 255

much less energy than before. I felt I literally needed coffee just to make it through the day and to function properly." Thankfully, after being awakened to the importance of proper nutrition and, even more so, by recognizing that there is correlation between mental health and physical health, he later reported to me some of the very real changes he had begun to implement within his daily life. "Jeremy, my mind was playing tricks on me because of what I was eating," he later said. You see, my friend, how can you possibly think that diet isn't directly correlated to the manifestation process within the law of attraction? The two aspects are so integrated and so interwoven that there is literally no separating the two. As we found in the book of James, a double minded man is unstable in *all* his ways. Such a man should never even *expect* to receive *anything* from the Lord. Diet is a very powerful aspect of the creative process because, more than anything else, it is a reflection of the inner mindset of the inner man. Do you want to see what people truly think of themselves? Simply look at what they're eating. Want to know what is truly going on within the mind of a man? Simply look upon the outside. You say, Jeremy, God doesn't look upon the outer man; he looks upon the heart? Well, my friend, just as it is from the abundance of the heart that the mouth speaks, it is also from the innermost part of the heart that a man chooses what to place into his body.

pg. 257

When I realized all those years ago just how vitally interconnected the mind and the body are, I immediately began to change my diet. Today, I find myself consuming primarily a vegetarian diet. It changed my life and not only impacted my clarity and mental state of awareness, but I have more energy in this season of my life than I did when I was a teenager. My friend, it is possible to renew the body by renewing the mind and becoming more conscious of what you are placing into your body – the temple of the Holy Ghost. How much more should a believer be a person of health than someone who does not believe? Along with preaching the power of divine healing, should the church not, even more so,

pg. 258

begin to preach the importance of living in health? The importance of making conscious decisions regarding diet and proper nutrition and proper exercise. My friend, if you truly want to begin manifesting the law of attraction in your life in order to attract the life you truly deserve, hear me when I say detoxify your body. You will never know the power of your own intentions until you are able to begin to think clearly – until your mind stops playing tricks on you. Diet is essential to powerful manifestation. As a student of the prophetic, I know, full well, just how interconnected health is to the patterns of God within the earth realm. Diet is essential to the power of the process of attracting because, quite simply, diet is essential to mental clarity and focus.

In order to better understand the importance of diet as it relates to mental clarity and focus, one needs only to examine the scripture and study the life of Daniel. In a time of Babylonian captivity, the children of Israel found themselves placed within a culture that was continuously trying to strip them of their true identities – much like today. We've all heard the story of Daniel being thrown into the den of lions, but did you know that part of the secret to Daniel's divine and supernatural power of attraction was his diet and eating habits? Yes, you read that correctly. According to

Daniel 1:8, the New International Version translation shares it this way: "But Daniel resolved not to defile himself with the royal food and wine, and he asked the chief official for permission not to defile himself in this way." (Daniel 1:8) Daniel did not wish to partake of the king's delicacies because the food of the king would have included foods that would have been forbidden under Mosaic law, according to Leviticus chapter 11. Much of the food had been offered to idols. In Daniel 1:12, Daniel instructs the ruler, "Please test your servants for ten days, and let them give us vegetables to eat and water to drink." By doing this, Daniel was quite literally drawing a comparison – comparing the diet of the king's men to the diets of the children of Israel. After the ten days had passed, not only was Daniel stronger and more agile than all of the king's men, but he had more mental clarity and sharpness. You see, my friend, one's diet is important in more ways than one. One's diet is directly correlated to either their honor or their lack of honor for the temple of God. Your very body is the temple of God. Are you honoring and respecting yourself through your eating habits and nutrition? If not, then begin to do so today. While in Babylonian captivity, in a strange land, Daniel was in essence saying to the king, "I will not live by the system of your world. I have a much higher calling."

pg. 262

If you find yourself still wondering what your diet and nutrition have to do with your power to attract the life you desire, well, let me say, quite frankly, that your diet is either a direct, outward reflection of your personal responsibility or your personal laziness. Yes, you read that correctly. I say that with all love and with all grace; however it needs to be said, now, in this season of manifestation, more than ever before. If you feel that your choices do not matter, then you are showing the world how truly lazy you are. To not be concerned with your diet and nutrition and overall health is to basically give up on life, in no uncertain terms. There is a very popular television program, now airing on television, which depicts the weight

pg. 263

loss journeys of what the medical profession terms as the "super morbidly obese." Many wonderful transformations of weight loss are documents in this popular program, as individuals not only lose weight but also begin to take control of their lives again. More times than not, though, along with the prescribed nutrition, counseling is also required. Why is this? Quite simply because even the medical profession understands just how deeply correlated and interconnected the mind and the body truly are. My friend, food can be used as either a source of nutrition to sustain you or as a drug and an idol – a form of suicide. As extreme as that analogy might see, it is absolutely true. By placing certain toxic foods

pg. 264

within your body you are essentially playing a deadly game of Russian roulette with your own life and your own well-being. Quite literally, with each and every delicious bite of toxic food you place into your mouth, you are placing another bullet into the chamber of an already loaded gun and taking a chance by pulling the trigger. As I was beginning to write this book, I sensed the Spirt say to me, "I want men and women to begin taking control of their lives, as I have designed them to." Today, a very real part of taking back control of your life is the decision to detoxify your body.

As we've discussed, everything begins with a conscious moment of awakening – a coming into a greater knowledge of truth. Now that you are beginning to recognize how vitally important your thinking is, as it relates not only to the decision making process but also to the manifestation of the physical life, you are awakening, consciously, to your own creative power. Today, begin to take the first step toward a more conscious way of living. These days, I focus completely upon organic, whole foods – foods of real color – when preparing my meals. You may feel that such selection is not worth the added cost; however, my friend, think of what it's truly costing you in the long run to not make healthy decisions and healthy choices? The end result could be quite deadly, in fact. For more than two millennia, the church has

pg. 266

preached the salvation of the soul – the saving by grace through faith – yet has literally, wholeheartedly promoted and endorsed the suicide of the body by not placing an emphasis upon health and wellness. My friend, when will you truly begin to take responsibility for your own life and your own actions? If not now, when? My friend, I say as respectfully as I know how, more than a revival of miraculous healing in the world, we desperately need a revival of good, old-fashioned common sense. More than a resurgence of the supernatural power of God within the earth, we need a resurgence of the power of accountability to ourselves and personal responsibility.

MASTERING THE DOMAIN

When I first began to ponder the significance of the power of the law of attraction within our lives, all those years ago, and when the Spirt of God first began to awaken me to the greater realities of the eternal correlation between what we think and what we see within our lives, I began to find myself often weighed down by what it all seemed to mean. To a mind that has just awakened, the idea of awakening to a more conscious creation can seem like such a heavy burden to bear. "You mean, I'm responsible for this life?" I so often found myself feeling anxious at what such a concept would even mean. Also, there was the very real fact that the idea of personal responsibility seemed to fly directly in the face of what religion teaches. Let's face it. According to the lies of religion, there is never any work. I mean, in all honesty, isn't that what the church has basically preached to the world for more than two millennia? That God, through Jesus, has literally done everything and that we are, somehow, just here within the world to witness to others and to exist, just getting by, until, hopefully soon, Jesus will return in the clouds? What a wasted life. What a wasted existence. It seemed like such bondage, really – the life

pg. 270

which religion had told me was my destiny. As the Spirit of God began to awaken me to the greater, revelatory truths found within the scriptures – the cycles and mysteries hidden within the text of the Word of God, I began to recognize, very early on, that the purpose of the life of the believer has always been a life based upon personal responsibility. Yes, it is the blood of Jesus which covers and which make all things new, but then what? What next? Is that the mere ending to the story? What about life? You see, as I was drawn into the deeper truths and mysteries of God and as the power of the prophetic voice began to be awakened and ignited within me, I realized that for far too long within Christendom, we have strived to carry

pg. 271

the cross of Jesus, rather than picking up our own crosses and carrying our own burdens. *My friend, not even once did Jesus ask that you take up his cross – he asked that you take up your own.*

The truth behind the law of attraction is, at its most core and fundamental level, a principle based entirely upon personal responsibility. You see, awakening to the greater knowledge of the truth of the laws of God being enacted within the universe, means, quite literally, that we begin to understand we have a very real role to play. We are not mere chess pieces being placed and maneuvered about upon the board of life by the hands of something or someone outside and apart from us. We are not the mere actors upon a stage, being forced to deliver the written words of a script we had no hand in writing. Not at all. In fact, nothing could be any further from the truth. Though it is Christ who is the author and finisher of our faith, we have always had a very influential role in creating the script, contrary to what religion has deceived us into believing for so long, because we are in him. Being awakened by the Spirit to the greater truths of the Law of Attraction can seem like quite the heavy burden – quite the cross – to bear. However, for a brief moment think of the opposite? Imagine the results of years spent with careless creating, not being fully conscious of the role that we play within our own lives each and every moment of the day. Imagine, for a moment, the life lived by chance. My friend, the life of carelessness is a much, much more heavy burden to bear, I can assure you. These days, I find myself traveling lightly – both literally and figuratively speaking. No longer do I find myself feeling weighed down by the burden of the universe. Rather, these days, I recognize that it is the universe which exists at my command. I recognize, daily, that it is my union with Christ – the Oneness of my true identity – which causes me to not only bend the universe to my will, at the power of my thoughts, but also to command the universe with my thoughts to align around me all things that I require to live the life of my dreams. This, my friend, is the call of God upon your life, as a creator and as a joint-heir with Christ. There is no separation. There is no disconnectedness. No longer do I find myself weighed down by the cares of the day. *I do not belong to the day – the day belongs to me.* My friend, how are you now finding your own role within your own world? Do you rise to meet each day with a sense of dread, hoping that things will one day get better? Or, like me, do you command the day? You do have a very real choice in the matter, you know. People often ask me about the principles I have taught throughout the years and they ask, "Jeremy, do these principles really change your life?" I often can only respond

pg. 275

with a laugh. I reply, "You have no idea." You see, I feel compelled to share these divine principles of the universal law of attraction not as some daily mantra or some force of positive thinking, only. No, my friend, I share these principles with the world because, in my own life, it was these principles which changed everything for me. I teach these not because these principles are things I believe; I teach these principles because these are truths that I know. There is very, very real difference between believing and knowing.

These days, I also travel quite lightly in a very literal sense, as well. My life is filled with travel and has been for decades. I find myself constantly traveling these days – not only for purposes of ministry but also for purposes of pleasure. I love travel. To me, there is nothing quite like being able to see the world around me – the beautiful canvas which the Creator has placed his brush upon. There is such beauty within our world. Sure, it's easy to think of all the bad within the world today, but what about the good? What about the beauty? Why not dwell on these things, instead? When I began traveling all those years ago, traveling to speak at conferences and to minister at various churches and venues to audiences all throughout the world, I realized just how difficult it is to travel with more luggage than I needed. Think about it, my friend. These days, so often, we

pg. 277

choose to pay more money – to spend more – just to be able to carry more luggage with us when we travel. It's quite the contradiction, if you truly think about it. Times of travel meant to be times of vacation – times of refreshing getaway – become nothing more than additional days of stress because of the baggage we feel we need to carry. As a professional traveler, let me assure you that you haven't truly felt stress, worry, and anxiety until you've found yourself on a strict time schedule, racing through the airport terminal, rushing to catch a connecting flight, carrying six or seven bags of heavy luggage. And the question is, is it really necessary? Of course not. Let's be honest with ourselves. For getaways lasting only a few days, we pack two or three weeks' worth of clothing. It's funny when you think that even when packing for travel, we seem to travel with a sense of fear and anxiety in mind. "Have I packed enough?" "Did I bring everything?" It's stressful to even think about, isn't it?

These days, if I find myself traveling for a week, I make it a point to consciously decide to carry only what is needed. For me, for a week-long trip, I choose to carry eight sets of clothes – one set of clothing for each day and only one extra, in case of an emergency. You would not believe the difference it's made within my life. Yes, something as simple as travel is made much more stress-free when we place our thoughtful minds to it. We carry so much baggage because of our unwarranted and unjustified fear of the unknown – both in the literal sense and in the spiritual sense. For a moment, think of just how much unnecessary weight we carry with us even in our own home-life. How much of what we have is truly needed? In truth, I would dare say that, if you were to be honest with yourself, you would say "Not much at all." We live in an age where convenience is our king. Because of this, practically everything within our society, within our modern culture, is crafted to accommodate and to give a sense of ease. From our gadgetry and high-tech gear to all of the added pieces of furniture we add simply for the purpose of

pg. 280

decorating, we spend lifetimes amassing things which, at the end of the day, we'll never be able to take with us when we go. In the Lord's prayer, Jesus gave the illustration of praying only for what was needed for the day. "Give us *this day* our daily bread." These days, however, we would much rather hoard, just in case. When the children of Israel had been delivered from Egyptian bondage and found themselves in the wilderness, the Lord provided food in the form of manna. Each morning, fresh manna was given. However, the people were instructed to only collect what they needed for the day. This is the underlying reference being made by Jesus as he prayed the model prayer, "Give us this day our daily bread." My friend, how very often have we stored up and hoarded to ourselves excessively, simply because of an innate sense of anxiety? Hoarding and storing up things in excess is based primarily in fear. It's the ego speaking and not the Spirit speaking.

A very real principle of the law of attraction, dealing primarily with the beginning stages of attracting, is to simply declutter. Declutter your home – the place of your daily life. I promise you, you would not believe what a difference making the decision to declutter would be. Once you make the decision to begin to declutter your home or car or office space, follow through. Quite often, many of us who travel so very often find ourselves practically living within our cars – in a literal messy state of existence. My friend, part of being successful means possessing a spirit of excellence. The Spirit of Christ is, in essence, the Spirit of excellence. Take time to have your car detailed. Throw away the trash which has accumulated around you. As simple and as elementary as it might seem, you would be surprised what such a simple step will do in literally changing the energy within your home, office, or automobile. I have a dear friend who, years ago, lived in excess. For him, all those years ago, it wasn't enough, it seemed, to have one of each designer suit; he felt the need to have two or three of each, just in case. Before

pg. 283

long he had amassed so much materialism, he found himself in a very real state of depression. When beginning to study my course on the law of attraction, he informed me that he quickly realized just how much of his "baggage" was completely unnecessary to his survival. He decided to give away everything that wasn't truly necessary and to keep only what he needed. He said to me, once, "Jeremy, I've never felt so free." Often times, much of our hoarding or our amassing of materialistic things has very little to do even with a sense of the potentially unexpected and even more to do with our own sense of pride. Unfortunately, within our time, there is such a desire to, as they say, "Keep up the with the Joneses." In other

pg. 284

words, to us, appearance is so often everything. This, my friend, is based entirely within pride and within the ego. I am a firm believer that the universe desires us all to have the very best of everything and just as much of it as we need. However, I am also a very firm believer that the universe never intended us to live outwardly from a place of pride - always wanting to show off our success to the world through our own sense of materialism. My friend, you have the power, even now, to have exactly what you want; however, this is why the power of the prophetic and the power of discernment are so very crucial and vital when dealing with the power of creation and the enacting of the law of attraction. Intentions matter, equally as much as thoughts do.

So, in order to begin to recognize the power of the Law of Attraction within your own, daily life – to begin manifesting more consciously to attract the life you truly desire – remember how vitally important it is to manifest from a place of authenticity, even within the home. Take time to declutter. Take time to throw away the trash and take time to give away to others what is truly unnecessary to you. Keep only what you need. In other words, to put it quite simply, reposition your home – realign your home – and establish a greater energy within your own domain. Do not hoard from a mindset of lack and fear of the unknown. Be mindful of your purchases and expenses. Yes, the universe desires you that you be successful in all areas of life, having only the very best of all things. However, the universe also desires that we manifest from an authentic intention and from a genuine place. In order to truly master the manifestation around you, begin by also learning to master your own domain – your own dwelling place. Tidy up. Pick up. Clean up. Come from a place of excellence. Want to know the mindset of an individual? Simply look at whether or not they keep their home clean.

The way in which you maintain your home or place of residence says much about you – not only to others but also to the universe. Are you honoring and taking pride in yourself? Does cleanliness matter to you? Is there organization within your home or office? My friend, even organizational skills say a lot about the energy you are manifesting and the signal you are sending out into the universe. My staff knows that the corporate offices of Identity Network must reflect a place of excellence in every way. Why? Quite simply because, all those years ago, Identity Network was birthed to share the principles of God within the earth realm, and the Spirit of God is a Spirit of excellence. I know, full well, that in order for

pg. 288

the company to attract abundance that the office spaces must be organized. There is absolutely no clutter. You see, the energy we project determines the energy we attract. What we give, we, in turn, receive. Being aware of this principle of the universe, truly, makes all the difference in the world.

Personal responsibility goes far, far beyond the thoughts we think and also the way we live our daily lives within the physical, human body. Personal responsibility also is a very real part of the way we choose to organize even the most intimate aspects of our daily lives. There is no escaping the power of the Law of Attraction even within our own homes.

Do you have a burning, innate desire to attract a new home into your life? Well, as simple and as elementary as it might seem, start by cleaning and organizing the one you've got. By taking pride in all matters of daily life and living life with a sense of excellence, we are literally beginning to attract consciously from a place of honor. How can we truly expect the universe to give us what we truly desire when we have refused to be good stewards of what we already possess? Do you wish to attract more things? Quite simply put, start by appreciating what you already have. There is such a divine and cosmic power contained within the attitude of gratefulness. By being thankful for what we have and by honoring and valuing what we

pg. 290

already have, we are sending into the universe a signal which says, "You can trust me with more." I promise you, my friend, the universe is listening, ever-so intently, waiting patiently to manifest for you the desires of your heart.

LORD OF ALL

When first beginning to ponder the creation of this book, within my mind, I felt within me such an innate hunger to bear to you, the reader, my soul. For decades, so many throughout the world have heard my teachings and have followed my ministry. Many throughout the years have become faithful supporters of the prophetic work and have partnered with us to help us take the gospel of Jesus Christ around the world through the release of powerful prophetic words. Millions of lives have been changed – impacted and awakened by the power of the Holy Spirit. However, so often I find myself being asked, "Jeremy, tell us more about yourself." The words of this book, in some small way, give a glimpse into my very own life in a very personal way, as never before. I share these principles with you, my dear friend, because I want you to know from my own experience that there is powerful truth found within the Law of Attraction. As I've said for years, thoughts truly do become things. When we change our thoughts, we change our lives. This is, at its most basic element, not only the underlying power of the Law of Attraction but, much, much more so, the truth of the kingdom of God within the this physical world – this three-dimensional world in which we currently find ourselves now experiencing the lives we were incarnated into. I've said for years that we are eternal, powerful, thinking spirits, here on this earth to have a human experience. Prophetically, I know that to be the truth.

It simply cannot be said enough that we are powerful, eternal, thinking spirits. However, somewhere along the way, though, we became forgetful. Because of this we, in turn, became fearful of the world around us. A disconnectedness and a sense of helplessness ensued – all because we had forgotten that we are masters within this dimension. Having been given all power and all authority in this dimension of creation, we chose, instead, to see ourselves as helpless. We created systems of religion because of this, in an effort to make ourselves feel more of a sense of control. But then, thankfully, Jesus came and by so doing revealed to a very forgetful humanity the very heart of God – a heart of creation. He then revealed to humanity that it possessed the same creative power, and, in flames of fire, the church was born. There were miracles, signs, and wonders and, for most, it seemed as though there was nothing more. However, for a few, select others, there came also the awakening of the spirit within. As His heart touched our hearts, we remembered that, in fact, His heart

pg. 296

was our heart all along. It always had been. It always will be.

There has always been what can only truly be described as a remnant – those who have refused to settle for the mundane mediocrity of lifeless, cold, stale and stagnant religion which seeks to keep us isolated and disconnected from the Godhead within our own minds. Somewhere along the way – somewhere throughout the journey – we allowed it to happen. We stopped seeking. We stopped searching. We simply settled. And by doing so we refused to change. We, in turn, began to seemingly fall prey to our own demises – merely victims within a world which seemed to control all the power, within a world in which it seemed the decks had been stacked against the whole of humanity. To us, for so, so very long, it seemed as though the sense of hopelessness we felt was forever meant to far outweigh the sense of hope and the sense of optimism. I realized long ago, my dear friend, that you are I were created for much, much more than what religion could ever convey. I write these words to you not only to share with you my very own story of awakening but, more so, to say to you that you've always possessed far more power than you could ever even imagine or truly comprehend. You are the creator of your life. No because you seek to be God but, rather, because through Christ, you simply are an

pg. 298

extension of the Creator within this earthly realm.

You see, not only is there more, the truth of the matter is that there is much more. There always has been. I continuously speak of awakening because, prophetically speaking, I know full-well that it is only through the awakening of the Spirit within – the true Spirit – that one can even begin to grasp the full measure of the innate power of creation, always lying dormant within. "I've called you to awaken the minds of your fellow creators," I sensed the Spirit say. A hunger was begun within me, all those years ago. A hunger to not only awaken but to awaken others. You see, at the heart of the universe lies a law of giving and receiving – a great law of interconnectedness. What we give out, we will forever be forced to, ourselves, receive. Awakened people awaken people.

Today, after all these years in ministry, the cry of my heart is twofold. I wish for the church which Jesus began to truly begin to be the church, rather than the primitive and archaic powerless institution we now see it settling to be within the world. Secondly, even more importantly, I am determined that I will manifest the power of the kingdom of God within the earth as a co-creator, just as he intended. For decades in prophetic ministry, I have done this and will continue to do this until I breathe my last breath upon the physical earth. Then, though, I will still continue to create. I will continue to create because, quite simply put, I have no choice in the matter. When the Spirit of God moved upon the face of the deep, long before time ever began, as the heart of the Creator moved to paint upon the great canvas of nothingness all the stars in the heavens, I was there with him. I do not simply believe this, my friend. I know this. You were there, too. You were with me. You and I were together, in him.

My friend, I share these truths not to in any way say that I have fully arrived. Each and every day, I find myself still being drawn into the greater mysteries of God – called forth into even deeper and greater waters of revelation. However, I wish to remind you of who you are. As a co-creator with God, you are, even now at this very moment, an extension of God - not only in this dimension but within all dimensions and space and time. Science has continuously and consistently proven to the entirety of the world the truth of the message of the kingdom – that the power to create has always been within – not without. Nothing has ever happened to you that you were not, in some very real way, a partaker in. I say this to you because I know, firsthand, the creative power of, both, the natural and the spiritual mind and the

pg. 302

sovereignty which is ignited when those two come together and are reunited as one.

I know that right now, to you, it might feel so very hopeless and so very discouraging. Feeling as though you are continuously being tossed about by mighty, restless and unsettled waves of the universe. You look to others and see that they seem to have it all together. You see their successes. You see their many great and varied accomplishments. In fact, you've seen many of those within your life climb the highest mountain tops and, seemingly, ascend to the highest pinnacles of success. You've then asked, "When will it ever be my turn?" You've pondered, "God, where are you?" My dear friend, as a prophetic voice, I serve only as a reminder to you of your true identity. If you wish to find God, I will lovingly hand you a mirror so that you might see His reflection staring back at you, through your own eyes. If you wish to see the great Creator, I will direct you to the looking glass so that you might see yourself, once again. I will lovingly and gently remind you that when you gaze into the mirror, it is the Creator you see, looking back at you, through your own eyes. Do you not yet see? How truly interconnected we truly are? How that even at our most intense feeling of separation and isolation and loneliness we could not be separated, even were we to ever truly try? This is the essence of the kingdom of God – one of absolute Oneness. My friend, not once has there ever truly been the existence of two separate wills – your will and God's will – there has only been a moment of forgetfulness. Jesus, our great co-creator and joint-heir came to remind us of that. Through his very own body, he showed us the power of our own minds – reminding us that the very glory he shared with the father was the very same glory that we also share with him.

Separation, quite frankly, is an illusion, based in the lies of forgetfulness. Today, though, as never before, I wish to remind you of who you truly are. Of who you, truly, have always been. My friend, have you not yet fully realized that when the scriptures – the chronicles of our journey together – speak of him, they are also speaking of us? Truly, as he is, so are we in this present world – and into the next. Together, we have taken a journey, through science and through spirituality and through metaphysics, back into the very heart of God – into the truth of Christ Jesus. That truth of his name is that the glory which he possessed from the very beginning is also the glory which you now possess. I wanted to include this chapter, to be able to speak to you as myself, to all of you who have supported my ministry and the work of Identity Network throughout the world all these years. I want you to hear from me, Jeremy Lopez, that not only are you awakening to the greater truths of the kingdom of God, day by day, but that you've always possessed far more power than you have ever truly recognized.   My friend, you do not have to live as a victim any longer. It's alright to let go of the past. Regardless of the trauma you've encountered on the journey thus far, I promise you that, as frightening as it may seem, you're safe in letting it go. It's weighed you down for far too long. You've allowed it. Today, why not begin to fully live by learning to take personal responsibility for your life? Why not begin to, right now, recognize the creative power which you've innately always known you've had?   Begin to use it to not only accomplish great exploits in the earth, but begin

pg. 307

to use it to create the life you've always dreamed of. The Lord will do nothing, except he first shows his servants the prophets. For decades, you've allowed me to speak into your life, passing onto you the words of the Holy Spirit, straight from the heart of the Father. I will continue to do that until my final breath. However, now, in this season, I invite you to begin using the power which you truly possess to begin manifesting the life you truly desire. My friend, you are not a victim of the universe. The universe is at your command.

ABOUT THE AUTHOR

Dr. Jeremy Lopez is Founder and President of Identity Network and Now Is Your Moment. Identity Network is one of the world's largest prophetic resource sites, distributing books, e-books, and teachings to a global audience. For more than thirty years, Dr. Lopez has been a pioneering voice within the prophetic movement and has been considered by many to be a leading authority within the arena of success coaching. Currently, his proven coaching techniques and strategies of life coaching are being implemented by various training institutes and faith groups throughout the world. Dr. Lopez is the author of more than thirty books, including *Abandoned to Divine Destiny* and *Prophetic Transformation*. He continues to travel and teach nationally and internationally. He has ministered prophetically to heads of business as well as heads of state, including Governor Bob Riley of the state of Alabama and Prime Minister Benjamin Netanyahu of Israel. Each year Identity Network receives thousands of requests from individuals throughout the world seeking the prophetic guidance of Dr. Jeremy Lopez.

ADDITIONAL WORKS

Abandoned to Divine Destiny

The God Element Within Dreams

Prophetic Transformation

The Power of the Eternal Now

And many more

pg. 310

Made in the USA
Columbia, SC
24 June 2019